NAPA VALLEY LAWMEN

—— and ——

OUTLAWS

Todd L. Shulman

THE
History
PRESS

Published by The History Press
Charleston, SC
www.historypress.com

Front cover, top left: California Highway Patrol officer Melvin Critchley, circa 1926. *Courtesy of the Napa Police Historical Society*. *Top middle*: Napa police officer Chuck Hansen inspects a shotgun used in an attempted murder. *Courtesy of the Napa Police Historical Society*. *Top right*: Napa police officer Chuck Holden inspects the scene of a break-in. *Courtesy of the Napa Police Historical Society*. *Bottom*: High schooler Don Self takes a turn with the radio in a squad car in front of the Napa Police Department with Chief Sherwood Munk looking on during Youth Day in 1956. *Courtesy of the Napa Police Historical Society*.

Back cover: The badge worn by St. Helena's first lawman, Marshal John Hall Allison. *Courtesy of the Napa Police Historical Society*. Napa police dispatcher Etta Crocker is shown in the dispatch center, which was in the basement of the police station, in 1973. *Courtesy of the Napa Police Historical Society*.

First published 2020

Manufactured in the United States

ISBN 9781467142366

Library of Congress Control Number: 2020932089

Notice: The information in this book is true and complete to the best of our knowledge. It is offered without guarantee on the part of the author or The History Press. The author and The History Press disclaim all liability in connection with the use of this book.

CONTENTS

Acknowledgements 5
Introduction 7

1. Charles H. Allen 9
2. John Hall Allison 13
3. Nathaniel E. Boyd 17
4. George Secord 21
5. Alexander Herritt 27
6. Edward Glos 31
7. Constance Joseph Dellamadalena 36
8. Melvin Critchley 42
9. Sherwood Munk 48
10. Kenneth Hively 53
11. Delph Rexroth 58
12. Chuck Hansen 64
13. Chuck Holden 69
14. Ken Narlow 75
15. Harold Snook 80
16. Richard Lonergan 85
17. Ken Jennings 93
18. K-9 Vem 98
19. Napa Central Dispatch 103
20. Napa Police SWAT 109
21. The Napa Police Football Team 116

Bibliography 123
About the Author 127

ACKNOWLEDGEMENTS

T his book is the culmination of years of research and preservation carried on by the Napa Police Historical Society. Two of the society's pillars are to preserve the history of the Napa Police Department and to educate the public about the unique history of the department. The artifacts and photographs collected and preserved by the society form the starting point of each chapter in this book. This book would not have been possible without the firsthand narratives captured by the society during its oral history project. Several chapters were also edited by subject matter experts in the Napa Police Department—special thanks to Gus Ulloth, Sarah Freeman, retired sergeant Ryan Cole and Seargeants Pete Piersig and Nick Dalessi. The digitized online collection of historic Napa newspapers created by the Napa County Library has also been an invaluable resource. Finally, I would be remiss if I didn't thank my in-house editor—my wife, Stacey—for her brutally honest feedback.

INTRODUCTION

The genesis of this book came in 2006; finding that no one at the Napa Police Department was tracking the department's history, I endeavored to start the task. I began collecting photographs for inclusion in what would become my first book, *Napa County Police*, which was a photographic history of Napa County law enforcement. During this collection process, I received the first couple of artifacts. In an effort to preserve these artifacts, and to ensure they would be kept in perpetuity, like-minded people and I started the Napa Police Historical Society (NPHS). The mission of the NPHS is three-fold: to *preserve* the unique history of the Napa Police Department, to *honor* former and current Napa Police Department employees and to *educate* the public about the rich history of the Napa Police Department.

The other spark for this book came from lunch. I was invited to join a group of retired Napa County law enforcement officers who got together once a month for informal lunches. I became friends with many of the former officers and enjoyed when they regaled me with "war stories" of their time on the force. I took mental notes on some of these stories, which would later become the starting point for this book.

Each artifact collected and preserved by the Napa Police Historical Society has a unique story to tell. For this book I've picked a handful of artifacts from among the thousands of items donated to the society during the past decade, as well as cherished keepsakes in family member collections. Each chapter starts with an image of the artifact, from which I endeavor to bring to life the people who used it through collected stories of those who owned the item and the infamous crimes they investigated. In addition to artifacts and images, I've brought these stories to life with the help of oral history interviews, interviews with surviving family members and documentation gleaned from local newspapers.

1

CHARLES H. ALLEN

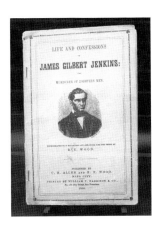

Charles H. Allen epitomized the character of the adventurous men and women who reinvented themselves in the wilderness of California in the 1840s. Charles Henry Allen was born in Rhode Island in 1817. At the age of twenty, he struck out, signing on as a deckhand on a sailing ship leaving from Connecticut and plying the Atlantic in search of elephant seals. These seals were sought after to extract oil, a crucial commodity since the most common illumination of the day was the oil lamp. Charles's ship made it to the Indian Ocean before running aground on a deserted island. Charles and his marooned shipmates spent fifty-two days on the island before being rescued by a French frigate that happened upon the forlorn crew.

Charles was not soured on sea life and promptly signed onto a whaling ship. The ship dropped Charles off on the island of St. Helena in the south Atlantic, off the coast of Africa. The island is best known as one of the most remote places on the earth and is where Napoleon was exiled in 1821. Charles presented himself at the U.S. consulate on the island; he

Above: This pamphlet was created based on the recorded confession of convicted murder James Gilbert Jenkins. It was published by Sheriff Charles Allen and R.E. Wood and sold for twenty-five cents. *Courtesy of the Napa Police Historical Society.*

This lithograph of Charles was created as part of his biography in the book *History of Napa and Lake Counties*, which was published in 1911. These biographical sketch books contained information paid for and provided by the people profiled themselves and were sold by traveling salesmen. *Courtesy of the Napa Police Historical Society.*

was bedraggled and beaten down by his months at sea. A biographical sketch that Charles later helped author described him as "ragged and barefooted." The consular gave Charles and his nine American shipmates one coin each and allegedly told them to go enjoy themselves. After walking around the island to the point that his feet bled, Charles once again sought help at the consulate and was given passage on a ship bound for Connecticut.

In 1849, Charles followed the flow of men hopeful to make their fortune in California at the start of the gold rush. When he arrived in San Francisco, Charles cashed in on his maritime experience by purchasing a small sailboat and loading it with cargo marketable to the newly arrived would-be miners. Charles sailed the ship up the Sacramento River Delta to the city of Sacramento, which was the jumping-off point for most of the aspiring miners. He sold the boat and its contents for a large profit and made his way to the gold fields of the foothills, seeking his own pot of gold.

It was during Charles's time in the gold fields that he first displayed his ability to be a peacemaker. He became known as a fair mediator when miners argued about claims. Charles served on several "miner's juries," part of impromptu and nongovernmental courts that formed in the vacuum of real government.

Charles came to the Napa Valley in 1853 to recover his health after a bout of fever. He never left. He reinvented himself again, this time as a farmer in

Browns Valley, an area immediately west of the city of Napa. Charles also owned a hardware store in downtown Napa for a time.

In 1857, Charles began his career of public service when he was elected to the County Board of Supervisors. In 1861, he was elected as Napa County's sixth sheriff.

It was during his time as sheriff that Charles worked on one of the most interesting murder cases in Napa County history. In 1862, James Gilbert Jenkins went to work for a rancher named Patrick O'Brien. Jenkins later claimed that Mr. O'Brien's wife proposed that they get rid of her much-older husband and take over his ranch as their love nest. Whatever the truth of his motive, in 1864, Jenkins went to a neighboring ranch and asked to borrow a rifle, professing that he needed it to hunt deer. Instead Jenkins set about hunting O'Brien, who was cutting down trees. Jenkins crept up to a ravine nearby, carefully aimed and took one shot, felling O'Brien. Jenkins then dug a shallow grave and buried his boss. An intense search resulted, during which Jenkins tried to throw searchers off the trail and steer them around the grave—to no avail. The body was found, and Jenkins was arrested by Charles and his deputy. A trial ensued; it took only a half hour for a jury of his peers to convict Jenkins and sentence him to death.

With the death sentence hanging over his head, Jenkins decided to unburden himself of his sins and warn others to avoid a life of crime. Charles sat with Jenkins in the jailhouse, and Jenkins dictated the confession of a life filled with crime. The result would become a pamphlet titled *Life and Confessions of James Gilbert Jenkins: The Murderer of Eighteen Men*. Jenkins was careful to clarify that although he murdered eighteen men in total, only eight of those were White men—the rest were Indians, an important distinction in Jenkin's mind. Jenkins detailed a litany of other crimes beside killing people, such as horse stealing and robbery, as he drifted from his childhood home in North Carolina across the country to California. Indeed, Jenkins claimed that he had decided to turn a new leaf and resolved to lead an upright life when he turned up in Napa County, only to be led astray by O'Brien's wife. Charles partnered with local publisher R.E. Wood to print the pamphlets and sold them for twenty-five cents apiece. Wood summed up the purpose of the pamphlet in its foreword: "The boys, especially of this coast, will do well to heed his warning, and have nothing to do horse-racing, gambling, whiskey drinking, or keeping bad company, for these will, as he said,—and every man of sound sense will sanction it—lead to crime, and it may be to the gallows."

Jenkins himself went to the gallows outside the county jail in downtown Napa on March 18, 1864. When the trapdoor was sprung, Jenkins fell, but his neck didn't break. Charles and his fellow onlookers waited thirteen minutes until the county doctor declared that Jenkins's heart had stopped.

After his stint as sheriff, Charles served as an officer in the Napa Guard (a precursor to the National Guard) and was elected to Napa's board of trustees, where he served as the city's treasurer. Charles retired from public service and returned to his Browns Valley ranch, where he died in 1896.

2

JOHN HALL ALLISON

John Hall Allison was a native Virginian, born just before Christmas 1827 to immigrant parents who had come to America from Ireland and Scotland. The Allison family moved to the Midwest and settled in Missouri.

John first made the dangerous trek to California alone in 1851. He spent one year in the Golden State and fell in love with it. Yet John was drawn back to Missouri to rejoin his first love, his fiancée, Susan. The couple settled down and had three children. Fifteen years later, after establishing himself as a successful farmer, John moved the family via wagon train to California. John was a natural leader who had experience crossing the frontier and was chosen to lead the wagon train.

John and his family settled in St. Helena in 1873. He built a house on Pope Street just east of downtown and had a twenty-acre parcel that he planted with grapes. The Allisons quickly became integral parts of the fledgling community and were charter members of the town's Presbyterian church when it was founded just a year later. John made such an impact on St. Helena that the street where his house stood was renamed Allison Avenue after his death.

Above: The badge worn by St. Helena's first lawman, Marshal John Hall Allison. *Courtesy of the Napa Police Historical Society.*

In 1876, St. Helena residents debated whether to incorporate as a city. A vote was held, and those favoring incorporation prevailed. The next step was to vote for the various elected offices, for the people who would run the fledgling town. A ticket of candidates was put together, consisting of prominent men who had supported the incorporation effort, including John, who threw his hat into the ring to be marshal. A second ticket was created with candidates who had all opposed incorporated but since that fight was lost had decided they wanted a say in how the town was born. When the election was held on April 10, John became St. Helena's first marshal; he won the vote by a two-thirds margin. All but one of the incorporation supporters won.

John's first job was constructing a practical jail to house his future customers. John got the job done for $158. In a testament to the quality of John's construction, the old jail stood for almost ninety years; it wasn't demolished until 1960. While no photographs of the jail in its heyday are known to exist, there is a fine watercolor of the building that was painted later in its life that still hangs on the wall at the St. Helena police station. Besides locking up law breakers, John's duties as marshal also included collecting taxes, enforcing the town's newly minted municipal code and being the town dog catcher. John wore another hat; during his time as a lawman, he did double duty as the town's superintendent of streets. It was his job to pilot a wagon along the city's streets, spraying water to reduce the dust kicked up by the horses.

John became embroiled in a tragic incident while off duty in September 1885. By this time John had hung up his badge and was serving as the town's elected justice of the peace. During this era, there were elected justices of the peace for each township in the county. They dispensed justice for petty crimes and civil matters in the communities they served. John discovered that a canvas cover for his buggy was stolen. He investigated and found it being used by several Chinese farmworkers who had fashioned it into a makeshift tent and were camping on a neighboring farm. Chinese laborers were employed throughout the Napa Valley for agricultural and manual labor tasks, such as excavating wine caves. Each town had its own Chinatown ethnic area, and many in the area had love-hate relationships with them.

John formed a makeshift posse; he and his two adult sons rode out to confront the thieves and retrieve their property. By this time, James, one of John's sons had already followed in his father's law enforcement footsteps and was serving as St. Helena's elected constable. The workers

Left: John as he appeared around the time he first arrived in St. Helena. *Courtesy of the Napa Police Historical Society.*

Right: John pictured during his tenure as St. Helena's justice of the peace. *Courtesy of the St. Helena Historical Society.*

weren't keen on relinquishing their shelter, and a brawl ensued, during which one of the workers grabbed a pole and swung it at John's other son, Johnny. John sprang into action, pulling his pistol and shooting the worker several times.

John immediately turned himself in to the sheriff but was released on bail. As an indication of how Chinese immigrants were regarded, the local newspaper that covered the incident never named the Chinese worker involved, instead referring to him only as a "Chinaman" or "Celestial." The *St. Helena Star* newspaper at the time pronounced its judgment on its pages, writing, "The case is clearly justifiable, as if the Chinaman had not been shot he would have killed Johnny. It won't take a jury long to dispose of this case and if they don't tender Judge Allison a vote of thanks for his swift punishment of the murderous Celestial we miss our guess."

A month later, Napa County district attorney Hogan arrived in town by train from Napa to hold a preliminary hearing. The Chinese worker had nearly fully recovered by this time but failed to show up to the hearing. He may have been encouraged to leave town by John's supporters. DA Hogan was more than happy to dismiss the case.

John held many positions of leadership in St. Helena. After his stint as marshal/assessor and justice of the peace, he became the director of the town's water company in 1886, as well as president of the local cemetery.

John died in May 1893 and is buried in the cemetery that he helped govern.

3

NATHANIEL E. BOYD

When people see photographs of Chief N.E. Boyd taken later in his life, the comment most often made is "that's Colonel Sanders!" Nathaniel Ellington Boyd was born in rural Russell County, Virginia, in 1848. He moved out West to California, settling in Sutter County, north of Sacramento, where he raised livestock and had a farm. Nathaniel married his first wife, Laura, in 1871; the union produced four children. Laura passed away unexpectedly in 1882 at the age of thirty; this left Nathaniel with four children, including an infant, none older than ten years old. Nathaniel married his second wife, Eleanor (better known as Nell), in 1890. The family moved to Napa around this time.

Nathaniel was a rancher and farmer for most of his life, coming to law enforcement just shy of his sixtieth birthday. He ran unopposed for town marshal of the City of Napa and was elected in 1907. During this era, there was no requirement that lawmen have prior legal training. Citizens voted for people who they deemed trustworthy and who were straight shooters. The marshal's term was two years, and most marshals served their term and then returned to their chosen profession or retirement. Nathaniel held

Above: This set of Tower brand handcuffs were carried by Chief Boyd during his career at the Napa Police Department. After he retired, he passed them on to the succeeding chief, Charles Otterson, who did the same in succession, until the 1970s, when Chief Ken Jennings took over the department. Chief Jennings donated the handcuffs to the Napa Police Historical Society before he passed away. *Courtesy of the Napa Police Historical Society.*

this position through 1909, when an act of the California state legislature abolished the elected marshal position throughout the state. Prior to that time, Napa's board of trustees would give the elected marshal the title of chief of police. Nathaniel made the decision to stay on and transitioned to being Napa's first full-time police chief. Throughout this period of his life, Nathaniel became known by his initials, N.E.

During Nathaniel's time at the NPD, his entire force consisted of two to three officers and himself. Nathaniel also employed a couple of night watchmen whose primary duty was to raise the alarm if a fire was detected—a very real and potentially cataclysmic proposition for a town built mostly of timber. During special events or holidays, he would employ special officers, citizens who were brought on as temporary help (akin to reserve police officers employed by some departments today).

In 1909, Nathaniel instituted the first "beat" patrol system. He assigned each of his two officers a specific geographic area of the town to patrol. At the time, the newspaper reported Nathaniel's marching orders to his officers by telling them to "arrest every person seen on the streets in an intoxicated condition; every person who upsets bicycle racks, or disturbs the peace in any way; every person riding bicycles on the sidewalks, and all auto drivers who exceed the speed limit." Today the police department has four geographic beat assignments for patrol officers and most recently added a sub-beat to specifically handle the increased activity in the revitalized downtown and Oxbow area of the city.

A souvenir booklet about the Napa Police Department was produced in 1913 and was sponsored by local businesses. The glowing description of Nathaniel read, in part, "N.E. Boyd, Napa's efficient Chief of Police, is one of our best beloved officials and is widely known throughout the state. Through the medium of human kindness, leniency where leniency is deserved, and a word of encouragement to those in need of it, Mr. Boyd has endeared himself to thousands."

Perhaps one of Nathaniel's greatest nemeses was not a hardened killer or serial bank robber but instead a diminutive woman named May Howard. May ran an infamous brothel on Clinton Street at the present-day intersection with Soscol Avenue. At the time, the area was at the far north end of downtown. During Nathaniel's time, May ran what was called a "house of ill fame." It was an open secret that she ran her brothel for over twenty years. Nathaniel and his fellow lawmen, most notably Napa County sheriff Edward Kelton, tried on several occasions to shut her down, to no avail.

Left: This photograph of Nathaniel was taken in the town of Marysville in the early 1880s, before he moved to Napa County. He sports his signature goatee, which he kept his entire adult life. *Courtesy of John Boyd.*

Right: Nathaniel's photograph was featured in a 1913 publication titled *Napa Police Department Souvenir*. It shows him at the end of his career, when he displayed the full-on Colonel Sanders look. *Courtesy of the Napa Police Historical Society.*

Nathaniel and Sheriff Kelton pushed a case in 1912 against May for "conducting a house of prostitution"; she was acquitted by a jury of twelve men. Failing to close the brothel with direct action Nathaniel changed tactics. On one raid in 1913 Nathaniel and his men found that she was keeping too much alcohol at her "rooming house." At the time there was a city ordinance that limited alcohol on hand to one quart per household. May was unphased and paid the twenty-five-dollar fine. In 1915, the lawmen tried a tactic of arresting two women housed by May for vagrancy, but more were waiting in the wings to take their places.

There is no doubt that the brothel drew an undesirable element, as evidenced in a wild incident in June 1916. Apparently, May denied entry to a rowdy band of young men, which they didn't take well. The men decided to use "vile epithets." May was a woman of action and was fiercely protective of her "girls." She retrieved a pistol from her bedroom and proceeded to let loose two wild shots in the general direction of the men on the street in front of her house. Not taking kindly to being shot at, the men proceed to pick up some loose bricks and lob them at the brothel. At that point, May

The former home of madam May Howard's brothel is razed to make way for the northern expansion of Soscol Avenue in 1978. Napa County sheriff Philip "Bucky" Stewart and Napa County district attorney James Boitano look on. In an ironic twist, Boitano was the home's last owner. *Courtesy of the Napa Police Historical Society.*

finally picked up the phone to call the police for help. Unsurprisingly, when Nathaniel detailed two officers to check it out, by the time they got on scene, the men were long gone.

This incident is a prime example of a saying common in police work: "You can't choose your victim." Lawmen take an oath to protect everyone, even those who might be criminals. May outlived Nathaniel's career in law enforcement, and her brothel wasn't shut down for good until 1937.

Nathaniel retired from the police department in 1921, after the initial stages of a heart ailment were detected. He moved to San Francisco, where he passed away of heart disease in 1925. He is buried at a cemetery in the city of Colma, just south of San Francisco. Colma has been the burial site of choice for San Francisco residents since the turn of the century. It is said to have more dead people than the living population and has taken on the nickname of the City of the Dead.

4

GEORGE SECORD

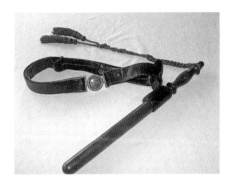

George David Secord was born in the California foothills town of Dutch Flat in 1856. By the age of fifteen, George's wanderlust wrested him away from the small town. He ran away to work in a series of lumber mills, earning $50 a month, plus room and board—quite a sum for the era. George squirreled away his earnings until he had enough set aside to purchase a team of four horses and a wagon, which he used to haul wood from the lumber mills to the burgeoning railroad construction industry. George was able to save an additional $4,000 (worth over $11 million in today's money). Unfortunately, George's father convinced him to invest the money in mine speculation, and George lost it all.

Undeterred by the mining fiasco, George sold his horse-and-wagon team and reinvented himself as a fireman for the railroad. George's job was to shovel coal into the maw of the steam engine's boiler. After three years of the backbreaking work, George opted for a much less taxing job as a clerk in a hotel in Auburn, a town on the road from Sacramento to the Sierra Nevada mountains. He moved to Napa around 1876, the year after the city officially

Above: This baton and belt were worn by George Secord while he patrolled the streets of Napa. The leather belt features a standard brass belt buckle with the word "police" embossed on it. Batons at the time were an individualized item. Many were handmade by the officers themselves. *Courtesy of the Napa Police Historical Society.*

formed its police department. He worked as a clerk in the two finest hotels in town, the Palace and Napa Hotels.

When the work of electrifying Napa was undertaken, George was hired as a lineman, climbing poles and stringing wire throughout the city. His work ethic was such that he was made the first foreman of the city's electric plant in 1890. That same year marked the start of George's long career in law enforcement.

George was elected as Napa Township's constable in 1890. During this period, each township in the county had its own constable who was elected to a two-year term. Constables reported to the town's assigned judge, working as a bailiff to keep the peace when court was in session and patrolling the town to keep the peace and augment the small police force. George served several terms as town constable, through 1906. In that year, Napa's board of trustees decided to appoint full-time police officers to fill out the ranks of what had been a police department on paper only. George received badge no. 1.

The virtues of being a police officer of George's era were perhaps best summed up in the 1913 *Napa Police Souvenir* booklet: "To the man in uniform who patrols a beat, falls the duty of preventing crime. It is he who makes or unmakes a police department. Detectives may be able to evolve mental processes of deduction which have as their aftermath the arrest of clever criminals, but it is the man who in slang parlance 'hoofs a beat' that upholds the majesty of the law. A police department is no better than the average of the men who do the quiet, unostentatious and prosaic work of routine."

George served with the Napa Police Department from 1906 until his retirement in 1915. While he spent a good portion of his time hoofing a beat on foot patrol, George was also known to use a single-horse buggy to get to the more far-flung areas of the city. His career of service to the citizens of Napa spanned twenty-five years. While it is somewhat common now for officers to serve twenty or twenty-five years in law enforcement, during the time George served, this was quite unusual.

Napa historian Louis Ezettie wrote about George in several of his Napa's Past & Present columns, which appeared in the *Napa Register* newspaper in the 1960s and '70s. In one article, Ezettie described how George enforced the curfew for underage Napans, which at the time was 8:00 p.m. in the winter and 9:00 p.m. in the summer. The night watchman rang the bell, which was in the cupola of the courthouse downtown, signaling the time when curfew had started. George took

George poses for a formal photograph, circa 1906. He wears the standard keystone cop–style felt helmet. When armed with a pistol, Secord would have carried it under his tunic, instead using the business end of his baton to persuade law breakers. *Courtesy of the Napa Police Historical Society.*

juvenile delinquents breaking curfew to the back of the firehouse, located on Second Street between Coombs and Randolph Street, for some on-the-spot justice; he enlisted them to manually pump water into a rooftop cistern at the building.

Throughout his time as a lawman, George also volunteered as part of Napa's Hook & Ladder Fire Company; Napa didn't have a full-time fire department until 1906, relying instead on several all-volunteer companies. These volunteer fire companies were more fraternal clubs than public safety groups. I can't help but think of the scene from the 2002 movie *Gangs of New York*, in which two rival volunteer fire companies get into a knock-down, drag-out fight over which will fight a fire at a tenement building. While there is no record of fire company brawls in Napa, there is no doubt that rival companies each considered themselves the best in town and competed to have the best-looking uniforms, the best firefighting apparatus and to hold the best social gatherings.

The reunion of members of the all-volunteer Napa Hook & Ladder No. 1 fire company are pictured in this 1918 photograph. George is third from the left in the front row. *Courtesy of Napa County Historical Society.*

Napa's Alden & Levinson semipro baseball team. George was the team's manager and is pictured in the center, dressed in a suit. *Courtesy of Napa County Historical Society.*

Another one of George's passions was baseball, and he managed several local amateur Class D teams over the years. In 1905, one of George's teams played an exhibition game against the Baltimore Orioles at a field in east Napa. The crowd was pegged at 10,000, a record for sporting event attendance in the county. It was even more incredible because the entire population of Napa County was around only 6,600 people at that time. The Napans lost by a small margin to the professionals.

I had the opportunity to conduct an oral history interview with George's nephew, Bani Scribner, in 2006. He fondly remembered as a young child tagging along with Uncle George as the burly cop walked his beat in downtown Napa. Scribner told a story of how George would fetch fresh apples from fruit stands along the sidewalk, pull out his pocketknife and skin the apples for Scribner.

George's health was in decline for several years after his retirement from the force, and he passed away in 1927, at the age of seventy, after a bout of pneumonia.

5

ALEXANDER HERRITT

Chief of Police Alexander "Sandy" Herritt presided over the Napa Police Department during a tumultuous time in the Napa Valley—the years when Prohibition was in effect. He took the post in 1923 with no law enforcement experience. Sandy was, however, an accomplished businessman and leader of men. He worked at one of Napa's tanneries as a superintendent. In the first half of the twentieth century, Napa was known for its quality leather goods production. The term "Napa Leather" became synonymous with high quality, and several tanneries dotted the shoreline of the Napa River. After working at the tannery, Sandy worked at the Mare Island Shipyard, in nearby Vallejo, as a civilian manager.

When Mayor Ralph Trower appointed Sandy as chief of police, the *Napa Daily Journal* newspaper reported, "Mr. Herritt is a citizen who has the confidence and respect of the entire community and it is anticipated that his administration will witness a vigorous enforcement of the city ordinances without fear or favor."

Above: This handsome fourteen-karat gold badge was presented to Chief Herritt in 1930. The inscription on the back reads "Presented to Chief A.F. Herritt by his friends, 1930." It was donated to the Napa Police Historical Society by one of Herritt's relatives. *Courtesy of the Napa Police Historical Society.*

Chief Alexander Herritt,
1927. *Courtesy of the Napa Police
Historical Society.*

At the time of his appointment, Sandy was quoted as saying, "I will give to the people of Napa the best that I have. That's all there is to it. Every effort that I can make to fill the office efficiently and to the satisfaction of this city will be honestly and conscientiously put forth."

It was rumored that Sandy's predecessor, Charles Otterson, resigned when he refused to arrest locals for alcohol-related offenses during the first few years of Prohibition. Sandy proved true to his pledge to enforce the law. In December 1924, Sandy and three of his officers raided what was known at the time as the Stonehouse, a business located at the corner of Main and Clinton Streets. The chief had arrested two Sonoma youths with alcohol, who in turn claimed to have purchased it from the Stonehouse. During the raid, a small quantity of wine was found in owner Charles Ceriani's possession. Sandy's instincts would later be proven correct, when Napa County sheriff Steckter found over two thousand gallons of wine at Ceriani's house in the Browns Valley area of town. In an ironic twist, the property that housed the Stonehouse has come full circle—for the last decade, it has been home to the Vintner's Collective, a wine tasting room for a group of fifteen small boutique wineries.

In fact, Napa's newspapers during Prohibition were replete with news of raids led by Sandy and his men at various homes and establishments in the area, including raids of "soda shops." With the passage of the Eighteenth Amendment, the myriad saloons that dotted downtown Napa were shuttered. Food historians have noted that throughout the country this spurred the explosion of soda shops, which acted as a replacement for men to congregate since the saloons were shuttered, and Napa was no different. Some of these soda shops sold purportedly legal beer. During Prohibition, beer with an alcohol content of under 1 percent was still legal. Sandy obtained samples from legal beers sold in town to ensure they complied with the law.

Sandy's commitment to uphold the law was tested in 1925. He and Napa County sheriff Joe Harris led yet another round of raids at suspected bootleggers' speakeasies. One of those caught in the dragnet was Joe Uboldi, one of Napa's finest. Officer Uboldi was a five-year veteran of the force at that point, and he held additional roles as one of the city's night watchman

This group photograph dates to 1928 and shows Chief Herritt (*seated, center*), with the entire force at the time. Present in the photograph are (*left to right*): Ed Moore, Julius Ojeda, Constance "Del" Dellamadalena, Chief Alexander Herritt, Dick Kermode, Ed Glos and Henry Anderson. *Courtesy of the Napa Police Historical Society.*

and the pound master (head of the animal pound). Sandy conferred with Mayor Charles Trower, who then fired Uboldi the same day.

Sandy's law enforcement career was cut short when he died unexpectedly in 1933. He was on duty at the time and had just pulled the police department's only patrol car out of the garage that housed it. At the time, the police station and adjoining garage were located on Brown Street, just across the street from the courthouse. Sandy only drove a short distance before being stricken by a massive heart attack. His patrol car rolled to a stop at the corner of Brown and Third Streets. Horrified onlookers rushed to Sandy's aid, calling for a doctor and then whisking him off to the hospital, to no avail. Sandy was later credited with saving lives even in death by taking the patrol car out of gear before collapsing, preventing it from possibly harming others as a runaway.

On hearing of Sandy's death, one newspaperman remarked, "The newspapermen of Napa had occasion to come in close contact with the chief of police. They knew him to be eminently fair and honest. They delighted in working with him."

Sandy's funeral literally brought Napa to a stand-still. A holiday was declared, and city government offices were all closed so that employees could attend the service. Napa Police and California Highway Patrol officers provided an honorary escort from the chapel to Tulocay Cemetery for the chief's burial. Sandy is one of only two Napa police officers who has died while on duty—both from heart attacks. Thankfully, no Napa County law enforcement officers have ever been killed by an assailant.

6

EDWARD GLOS

If you were driving through downtown Napa in 1960, you would have seen Ed Glos. He was the older nondescript gentlemen with silver hair and spectacles riding a three-wheeled Harley-Davidson motorcycle. You would have seen him making his rounds and collecting change from the parking meters that dotted the streets and parking lots. You would have had no idea that Ed had a long and storied life as a soldier, a two-wheel pioneer and a lawman.

Ed's parents, Charles and Anna Marie, were German immigrants who met in San Francisco. Charles was a butcher, and after the first two children were born, the Glos family moved to Napa County. Edward "Ed" Glos grew up in the wilds of the Napa Valley on a hillside farmstead outside Calistoga that his parents founded in 1885. Ed was born in 1892; the family's first home was a log cabin with packed sand floors. The family

Above: Ed Glos's service weapon of choice was a Smith & Wesson .38-caliber revolver. At some point during his time at the police department, Ed befriended an inmate at the county jail who happened to be a master engraver. The inmate, whose name is lost to history, took Ed's prized revolver and added engraved scrollwork and Ed's name, "E.J. Glos." Many years later, Ed's daughter, Dorothy Soderholm, loaned the revolver to the Napa Police Historical Society, and it was displayed with pride in a case in the public lobby of the police department. *Courtesy of the Napa Police Historical Society.*

eventually moved to the St. Helena area so that Ed and his nine siblings could attend school.

Ed's first job was as a delivery driver for the Napa City Bakery, and he was later a chauffeur. Many citizens hadn't learned to drive during the early decade of the automobile, so the job of chauffeur was common. Like many young men, when war broke out across the pond in 1914, Ed felt pangs of patriotism and the call to do something.

When the United States finally entered the fray of World War I in 1917, Ed answered the call of public service; at the age of twenty-five, he enlisted in the Napa Ambulance Company no. 1. Instead of being sent to the trenches of France, the unit was sent to the Mexican border during the skirmishes near Nogales, Arizona, which were part of a larger border war carried on between Mexican army and militia troops and the U.S. Army. This was Ed's first foray on two wheels, riding a motorcycle during the conflict. It would foreshadow his long future both personally and professionally on two wheels. After Nogales, he was sent to Camp Kearny in San Diego County, where he trained other U.S. Army medics, preparing them for deployments overseas.

For many years after his military service, Ed ran a successful bicycle business, Napa Cyclery, which was located at the corner of First and Coombs Streets. As was common during this era of motorcycle development, Ed sold and serviced both bicycles and motorcycles. Indeed, the first practical motorcycles were just that: cycles modified with small motors. Ed became a police officer in 1930. In keeping with Ed's love of all things two-wheeled, he had the distinction of being the Napa Police Department's first motorcycle officer.

One of the most interesting cases Ed was involved in occurred in 1933. There had been a series of child molestations that had occurred west of downtown Napa. The heinous nature of the crimes, and the fact that they happened in the then-sleepy hamlet of Napa, shocked the whole town. Everyone was on edge, and everyone was looking to the police for protection. Ed was one of a squad of officers detailed by the chief of police to stake out the area where one of the attacks had occurred, Jefferson Street near the Napa Creek, in hopes that the suspect would return. Ed was hiding in a shrubbery on the banks of the creek when a man walked toward him along the creek bed; the man's clothing matched what the suspect had been wearing during a prior attack. Ed sprang from his hiding spot, flashed his badge and ordered the man to stop. The man, later identified as Ray Lanham, squared up and appeared to reach for a pistol in the waistband of his pants. Ed drew

Ed is pictured on an Indian motorcycle with sidecar while serving with Napa Ambulance Company no. 1, circa 1918. *Courtesy of John Martin & Danie W. Hancock.*

Napa Cyclery, which Ed owned before joining the Napa Police Department. *Courtesy of the Napa County Historical Society.*

Ed sits astride his Harley-Davidson police motorcycle in 1933. He wears a six-pointed silver star on his uniform. This badge was the model used when the Napa Police Department issued a commemorative badge for its 125th anniversary and is the style worn by officers today. *Courtesy of Dorothy Soderholm.*

his service revolver and pulled out his blackjack (a small leather baton with lead sewn into its end), ready for whatever came his way. Lanham instead took off running, clambering up the embankment and crashing through the fences of three houses. Ed was hot on his heels. As Lanham got to his fourth fence, Ed fired a warning shot into the ground. Lanham was undeterred and started to mount the fence. Ed's revolver barked twice more. Both slugs hit home, striking Lanham in the hip and leg.

Lanham continued another city block, with Ed in hot pursuit, now blowing frantically into his police whistle. (This was the era before handheld police radios). Two citizens heard the commotion and came to Ed's aid before his fellow officers could. The three men were finally able to overpower Lanham and slap the cuffs on him.

After Lanham was subdued, a makeshift replica pistol, made of wood and wrapped with electrical tape, was found hidden in Lanham's pants pocket. He was rushed to Napa's Victory Memorial Hospital, suffering from the gunshot wounds, one of which caused extensive damage to his intestines.

The newspaper the next morning reported that doctors gave Lanham a "1 in 100" chance of survival; however, defying the odds, he did pull through.

In the next morning's newspaper, Police Chief Eugene Riordan summed up his assessment of Ed's actions: "I have nothing but praise for the actions of Police Officer Ed Glos and I am sure that the citizens of this community, especially the parents of small children, will stand squarely behind the actions of the police department in its treatment of the case."

After his recovery, Lanham was found guilty at trial and was sentenced to twelve years in prison.

Ed's years as a cop ended in 1946. Like many before and after him, Ed couldn't completely walk away from the police department he had come to love. For many who pin on the badge, being a cop is a career—not just a job. The relationships that officers build with each other is strong; they are people who they have to literally trust with their lives. Ed tried for a time to not be a cop, working as a driver for the Noyes family at their ranch, located at First and Jefferson Streets, but he was drawn back to the police department. Ed took a part-time job collecting change and serving as the parking meter maintenance man. He was a fixture around town for over a decade more, riding a Harley-Davidson servi-car three-wheeled motorcycle. He fully retired in 1961.

Ed passed away in 1972, at the age of seventy-nine.

7

CONSTANCE JOSEPH DELLAMADALENA

C onstance Joseph Dellamadalena was a native Napan, born in 1891. His birth name was Constano. Like many children of immigrants who wanted to fit in, his name was later Americanized to Constance. He followed in his father's footsteps by farming their land in the Knoxville area in northeastern Napa County. The Dellamadalena family joined a thriving Italian immigrant population who flocked to the Napa Valley in the late 1800s. These were hardworking families who were seeking their American dream. The city of Napa itself had a thriving Italian American enclave north of downtown, next to what was known as Spanishtown.

Constance married fellow first-generation Italian American Lena and moved to Lyon County, Nevada, to farm some property his father had purchased; after several years, the family returned to Napa. Constance became a teamster (truck driver) before joining the Napa Police Department in 1925.

Above: This whistle was carried daily by Constance Dellmadalena. Before the advent of two-way portable radios, a whistle was a key part of a police officer's uniform. It was the primary means of calling for help. It was donated to the Napa Police Historical Society by Constance's granddaughter. *Courtesy of the Napa Police Historical Society.*

The criminal incident in which Constance suffered his most serious injuries didn't happen at work but as he slept peacefully at his own house. In 1936, an assailant burst into Constance's bedroom in the middle of the night. Constance groggily sat up and was punched in the face. He could not see his assailant in the darkened room and asked who it was. In response, the assailant immediately began beating Constance, pummeling his torso. Constance wound up heavily bruised, with three broken ribs.

It is every cop's worst nightmare: a criminal finds out where he or she lives and comes to take revenge for perceived injustice or poor treatment. When I started doing research on former officers, I was surprised to learn that until the 1960s, the local phone book routinely included the profession of those listed, including police officers. In addition, newspaper articles

This photograph of Constance dates from sometime in the 1930s to early 1940s. The date is based on the shield-style badge pinned to Constance's uniform. This style was only worn for a brief period. The shoulder strap present with the police belt also helps date the photograph. *Courtesy of the Napa Police Historical Society.*

announcing the hiring of new police officers regularly including the officer's home address.

In this case, however, the assailant turned out to be Constance's own brother, "Midge" Dellamadalena. Midge and Constance had been locked in a protracted family dispute about the Nevada property that had belonged to their late father. Midge was arrested by other officers; however, there is no record of what happened with the criminal prosecution. It is possible that the case was dismissed since it was a family matter, and it is doubtful that Constance would have pushed to have Midge locked up.

In 1941, the new year started with a mundane call for Constance. In the wee hours of January 1, a burglar alarm at the Napa Steam Laundry was phoned into the station. The business was located at the north side of downtown Napa. Cops routinely deal with burglar alarms, 99.9 percent of which turn out to be false. They regularly find alarms caused by absentminded employees leaving for the night, oscillating fans and feisty rats. Constance quickly learned this was one of the 0.1 percent. When he pulled up to the business, he could see two cash registers sitting outside the wide-open front door. Before he could call for backup, Constance heard something moving inside. He drew his service revolver and entered the business. Constance slowly crept into the darkened entry. He began methodically searching each of the small rooms on the first floor. He came to one man cowering in a storage closet while two others ran out a side door, hopped into a car and sped away. The unlucky suspect captured by Constance said his name was Gene Crosby and that he was from Yuba City.

Constance put out an all-points bulletin for the car that fled. Some alert cops in the city of Roseville, just northeast of Sacramento, found the car later that morning and arrested Crosby's compatriots. The case quickly expanded when Crosby confessed to a string of break-ins at businesses throughout the central valley of California and led authorities to several caches of stolen loot.

Constance's arrest of Crosby took on a new level of importance when the Napa police received a phone call from the FBI; Crosby was a wanted fugitive who had been on the run for six years after running afoul of the law in New Mexico and Texas.

Charles Walker was a taxi driver in Clovis, New Mexico, a sleepy little town on the border with Texas. The taxi company was a family business, where his wife took the phone calls from would-be riders, and Walker was the lone driver. On the night of February 21, 1935, Walker was summoned from home at 8:45 p.m. to pick up a fare at a local restaurant. He picked

Above: This 1949 photograph shows Constance (*left*) at the tail end of his career, while serving as the department's sole captain. He is standing with Officer Elmer Stahl in the area of the police station that was located on Brown Street, across from the old courthouse. *Courtesy of the Napa Police Historical Society.*

Right: Constance's son Frank Madalena is pictured in this 1970 department photograph. Frank had a long and successful career at the Napa Police Department and retired in 1975. *Courtesy of the Napa Police Historical Society.*

up two men who promptly pulled revolvers and forced Walker to drive five hours south, to the outskirts of El Paso, Texas. The men told Walker that they were part of a notorious prison break that had happened four days earlier in Granite, Oklahoma. Thirty-one prisoners had tried to escape, killing a guard in the process; eighteen made it out and melted into the countryside. As the taxi neared the city, the kidnappers ordered Walker to pull over. They bound, gagged and blindfolded him and then dumped him on the side of the road. Walker was able to free his feet and walked to a nearby highway for help. Walker's taxi was found later, stuck in a sand dune near the Rio Grande River. The location of the taxi led credence to the theory that the men were part of the prison escapees and that they sought the safety of Mexico.

Flash-forward to 1941, when G-men drove to Napa and interviewed Crosby at length in jail. He folded and confessed to kidnapping Walker six years prior. He told the agents that his accomplice on that caper, Jose Armento, had been shot and killed by the San Francisco Police Department when he tried to break into a jewelry store. Crosby was picked up by a duo of U.S. marshals and returned to New Mexico to stand trial for the kidnapping across state lines.

This whole episode is a prime example of how cops typically don't know who they're pulling over or contacting during calls. The person could be an average citizen who will apologize and be respectful, a down-on-their luck first-time crook who knows they've been caught and follows the cop's orders or a hardened criminal who believes that he or she has nothing to lose by assaulting the cop to escape at all costs.

At some point in the 1940s, Constance decided to further Americanize his name by dropping the first part of his last name, changing it to Madalena; his children followed suit. In fact, Constance had taken on the nickname Del during his time at the police department. Throughout his career, people knew him as Del or C.J. Constance and Lena had four children: Ralph, Frank, Rose and Virginia.

Constance served in the police department as it transitioned from a small division, serving during the tail end of Prohibition, to a larger force that had to adapt as Napa's population skyrocketed during World War II. During his tenure, the department acquired its first radios that were mounted in the patrol cars.

The (Della) Madalena family is a good example of the family nature of the Napa Police Department and the entire Napa law enforcement community. Three years before Constance retired, his younger son, Frank,

This badge was presented to Constance upon his retirement. On the back is inscribed "Presented to C.J. Madalena by the City of Napa, Calif." *Courtesy of the Napa Police Historical Society.*

took the oath of office and joined the force. Law enforcement families continue to this day at the department. At the time of this writing, there are several second-generation and one third-generation Napa police officers serving at the department, as well as one third-generation officer. In addition in Napa County law enforcement, there have been several married couples, siblings and cousins.

Constance retired in 1951, after serving twenty-seven years and rising through the ranks to captain. At the time, there was only one captain on the force, and he answered directly to the chief. Following his retirement, Constance went to work as a security guard at the Basalt Rock Company, located at the south end of town.

As in many families, cancer struck the Madalena family in 1955, when Constance's eldest son, Ralph, died at the age of thirty-seven. Unfortunately, cancer struck again in 1963, when Constance passed away after a hard-fought battle with the disease.

8

MELVIN CRITCHLEY

A book about iconic Napa lawmen would not be complete without a chapter highlighting the life of California Highway Patrol officer Melvin "Mel" Critchley.

Mel was born in 1905 in Elko, Nevada. His father, Thomas, had emigrated from England in 1876 and took up the newly created trade of electrical engineering. The Critchley family moved to California in 1922 and settled in St. Helena, where Thomas set up a trucking business. Mel and his older brother Jim's first jobs were working for their father. In 1925, Jim was the first to join Napa County's traffic patrol. This predates the formation of the statewide highway patrol. There was a hybrid model in which the state provided funds to each county, and each county sheriff was responsible for hiring and supervising the traffic officers, known as speed cops. The statewide California Highway Patrol (CHP) wasn't formed until 1929.

Mel's chance to join his brother came after tragedy struck. Only three months after Jim started patrolling, he and the only other traffic officer, Ramon Asedo, were off duty taking turns riding in a two-seat, single-engine airplane that their friend Dr. Roy Hunt owned. They were taking

Above: This vintage speed cop cap displays the hat piece worn by Melvin Critchley. At the time, each county had a unique hat piece. *Courtesy of the Napa Police Historical Society.*

off and landing at a baseball field in east Napa. It was Ramon's turn, and they were coming in for a landing when one of the wings broke off. The plane crashed to the ground and burst into flames as the horrified Jim looked on. Hunt and Ramon were both killed. After Ramon's untimely death, Jim was promoted to captain, and Mel filled the newly opened officer post.

Mel later recalled that one of the only requirements to join the force was the ability to ride a motorcycle. Applicants were also supposed to be twenty-one years old; however, as Mel told it, he was twenty at the time, but no one asked his age. In those early years, officers would ride a motorcycle issued by the county patrol during daylight hours, but at night, they were required to switch to cars. There were no patrol cars at the time, so each officer had to drive his own car and received a reimbursement of ten cents per mile driven. Mel's starting salary was $150 a month. Mel invested in a 1928 Studebaker roadster, spending $2,100, which was quite a sum for that era. The car had a top speed of ninety miles per hour, and Mel would later boast that he never lost a speeder while driving the Studebaker.

Mel only fired his duty weapon twice during his long career. The first time came in early December 1936. Humboldt County sheriff Arthur Ross was driving two prisoners to San Quentin State Prison to start serving their sentences. This included a twenty-one-year-old convicted burglar named James Anderson. As an indication of how lax Sheriff Ross considered the transport, he had his adult daughter drive the car while he chatted with the prisoners. When they got to the city of San Rafael, Sheriff Ross took the prisoners into a restaurant for lunch, and Anderson had other plans. When Sheriff Ross unhandcuffed Anderson, he promptly bolted for the exit. Anderson stole a car from the parking lot and was long gone before the stunned sheriff could call for help.

Anderson made his way toward Napa County and ditched the stolen car on Old Sonoma Road, the artery between Sonoma and Napa Counties. By this time, it was around 4:00 a.m. Already alerted to the escapee and his description, Anderson made the mistake of crossing paths with Napa police officers Dick Kermode and Jule Ojeda near Third and Main Streets in downtown Napa. Anderson fled on foot, losing the officers in the darkened County Courthouse Square. More officers were called, but after an extensive search, they came up empty-handed.

Mel decided to check the roads out of town to see if Anderson escaped the downtown area. Mel hopped into a patrol car with Napa under-sheriff Gaffney behind the wheel. Sure enough, as the duo drove near the

Mel posed for this photograph shortly after being hired as a traffic officer in 1926. *Courtesy of the Napa Police Historical Society.*

Old Adobe on Soscol Avenue, they saw Anderson duck behind a nearby gas station. Mel jumped from the still-moving patrol car armed with his sawed-off shotgun, yelling for Anderson to stop. Anderson was having none of it and sped up. Mel closed the distance by peppering Anderson with three rounds of birdshot. Bloodied but not beaten, Anderson was able to scramble away.

Anderson finally gave up several hours later. He had climbed down into a small creek near Imola Avenue and hidden in some scrub brush. He yelled to some officers who were searching nearby, "Come and get me. I'm tired!" Anderson was taken to the hospital for treatment, where he remarked to Mel, "I wish you had killed me" as the doctor plucked the twenty pieces of birdshot from his body. After being patched up, Anderson was taken to his new home at San Quentin State Prison.

The incident later became a joke during Mel's retirement party. It was pointed out that Mel, an avid hunter, had birdshot loaded instead of the standard buckshot carried by officers. If Anderson had been hit with three rounds of buckshot, he may not have fared as well as he did.

Mel and Jim both had long careers at the CHP, but Mel outstayed Jim by over a decade. Jim retired in 1954 and became a driver's training instructor at local schools. Mel and Jim's brother, Al, also had a long career of public service as a civilian firefighter at the Mare Island Shipyard in Vallejo.

At the end of his career, Mel no longer patrolled the streets of Napa County. He performed a series of administrative duties, including being the liaison between the patrol and the district attorney's office, inspecting school buses for mechanical issues, testing newly appointed school bus drivers and performing inventories of the patrol's vehicle fleet to make sure each car had the needed equipment.

Mel served over forty years with the CHP, all in the Napa office. In 1968, he was forced to retire when the State of California changed its mandatory retirement age to sixty. At the time, he was the most senior officer in the whole state, wearing badge no. 1. Mel told a reporter from the *Napa Register* newspaper, "It took an act of the legislature to get rid of me. I have enjoyed my many years in law enforcement and haven't regretted it." At Mel's retirement party, the deputy CHP commissioner announced that Mel's badge would be retired with him and installed in a place of honor at the CHP Museum, located at the CHP Academy in West Sacramento. In another tribute that was less formal but from the heart, staff from the school district Mel kept safe used watercolor paints to adorn Mel's pick-up truck with a hand-painted CHP logo.

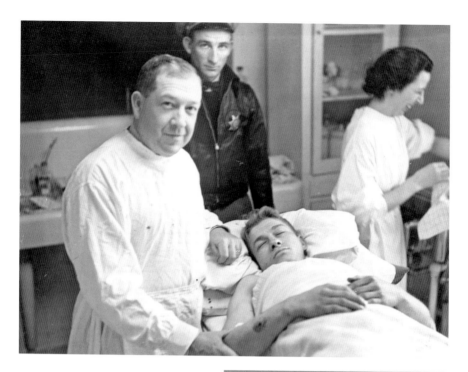

Above: A doctor at Napa's Parks Victory Hospital treats captured escapee James Anderson. Mel can be seen in the background, guarding his prisoner. *Courtesy of the Napa Police Historical Society.*

Right: In 1969, Mel posed for this photograph at the *Napa Register* newspaper's office for use as part of his retirement article. *Courtesy of the Napa Police Historical Society.*

After Mel retired, he continued his regular hunting trips back to Elko. He and his wife, Anna, were gifted sets of golf clubs when Mel retired, and they stayed active golfers during his retirement. Melvin died of a heart attack in 1980.

9

SHERWOOD MUNK

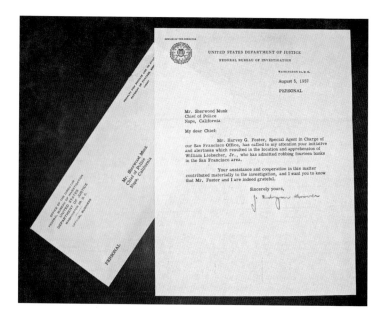

Sherwood Munk was a Napa native who was born in 1912. He started working for the city in the Water Department as a laborer. In 1936, he switched to the police department and was appointed as an officer. Sherwood worked his way through the ranks for the next fifteen years.

When I interviewed Sherwood's widow, Ruth, in 2006, she related to me that the only time she felt scared for her husband was during World War II. During the war, sailors and shipyard workers from nearby bases in the city of Vallejo would come to Napa to blow off some steam. Sherwood patrolled the many bars that dotted downtown Napa paired with U.S. Navy shore

Above: This letter from Federal Bureau of Investigation director J. Edgar Hoover was sent to Chief Munk in 1957, thanking him for his assistance in capturing a prolific bank robber. Chief Munk carefully preserved it in one of the many scrapbooks he compiled during his tenure at the Napa Police Department. *Courtesy of the Napa Police Historical Society.*

patrol personnel. Ruth told me a story of one night when Sherwood came home with his uniform shirt in tatters—the result of one of the many bar fights he broke up that night. Sherwood and his colleagues would break up the brawls and then order the combatant to walk one block to the nearby police station and wait to be booked at the jail or turned over to the Shore Patrol, and most did as they were told. In 1952, Munk took over as chief of police when the former chief, James Neel, left after only one year on the job to take the top cop job in Modesto.

Two of Sherwood's four sons followed him into law enforcement careers, a testament to the love of the job that he instilled in them. James became a Napa County sheriff's deputy. Richard became a police officer at the South Lake Tahoe Police Department.

Sherwood was an innovator who oversaw many positive changes in the department. During his tenure, he hired the first women to wear Napa Police uniforms: two parking enforcement officers who stepped in when needed to search female suspects and take custody of children affected by crimes. They were unarmed. These women proved themselves many times over and paved the way for the female police officers who would come later.

Sherwood sought to build ties with the children of Napa. He started a program each year in which a high school student would be Chief for the Day, shadowing Munk as he performed his duties. Sherwood also approved the formation of the Junior Traffic Safety Patrol (JTSP) in Napa.

Another program that Sherwood brought to the police department was the Reserve Officer Program. Started in 1958, the program recruited male citizens who had full-time jobs but wanted to help part-time at the department. These unpaid officers received abbreviated training and would patrol partnered with full-time officers. The reserve program was a formalization of the prior practice of bringing on special officers from time to time as events warranted extra help.

Sherwood was proud of his profession and the work done by the men and women of the Napa Police Department. An expression of this pride can be found in the dozen or so scrapbooks that he created during his time at the police department. He started these in 1936, with a photograph of Sherwood in his new uniform and an article about his own hiring. He religiously clipped newspaper articles and saved documents related to the police department. When I started the Napa Police Historical Society in 2006, Ruth donated the scrapbooks to our collection. Besides clippings, I found several treasures tucked inside the scrapbooks, including a hand-signed letter from the FBI's J. Edgar Hoover; copies of the city's annual

Above: A group of officers assembled at the police station on Brown Street in 1949. Chief Munk is second from the right. Protective body armor had not yet been developed for law enforcement. The officers pictured are wearing thick leather jackets and, in Chief Munk's case, an Ike jacket (styled after the jacked Dwight Eisenhower wore during World War II). The officers pictured are (*left to right*): Elmer Stahl, Delph Rexroth, Sherwood Munk and Howard Westendorf. *Courtesy of the Napa Police Historical Society.*

Opposite, left: Sherwood Munk as he appeared when he joined the Napa Police Department in 1936. *Courtesy of the Napa Police Historical Society.*

Opposite, right: This photograph of Chief Sherwood Munk was taken when he was sworn in as chief in 1952. *Courtesy of the Napa Police Historical Society.*

Opposite, bottom: High schooler Don Self takes a turn with the radio in a squad car in front of the Napa Police Department, with Chief Munk looking on during Youth Day in 1956. *Courtesy of the Napa Police Historical Society.*

report from the 1950s, which were pamphlets produced with updates from each of the city's departments; and several photographs.

Sherwood's life came to a tragic end in May 1967. Ruth left home at 8:00 a.m., as usual, for a part-time job. When the chief didn't show up to work, Detective Mike Silvestri was sent to his home to check on him. What met Mike at the house was something that would haunt him for years to come. Sherwood was found lying in the kitchen mortally wounded from a shotgun blast. He was wearing his business suit, as if he was ready for work, and was still clutching his department-issued shotgun.

There were several theories why Sherwood took his own life. One centered on his contentious relationship with the domineering city manager at the time, Lee Roberts. The city manager was known to listen to the police scanner at all hours and randomly drive around town to ensure that officers were doing their jobs. Sherwood and Roberts argued on several occasions about how the chief was running the department and about officers who Roberts thought should be fired. The ironic part of this theory was that Sherwood didn't have to still be working in 1967. He was due to retire in 1966, but Roberts convinced him to stay on another year while they searched for a new chief.

Ruth had her own theory, which she shared with me before she passed away. At some level, she still refused to believe that her husband would take his own life. She recounted to me a confrontation the chief had with an unknown man in their front yard a week before the chief died. She implied that the man had killed Sherwood and staged the scene to look like a suicide.

Sherwood was afforded a full law enforcement funeral, including pallbearers from the department he dedicated his life to. Law enforcement officers from the community and nearby areas attended to pay their respects to a man who spent his entire adult life in public service to the citizens of Napa. Photographs from the funeral show lines of law enforcement and members of the Junior Traffic Safety Patrol lined up outside the chapel to honor Chief Munk.

10

KENNETH HIVELY

Kenneth Mann Hively was a native of Long Beach and was born in 1916. Like many lawmen featured in this book, be felt the pull of public service early in life. In 1932, at the age of seventeen, he enlisted in the U.S. Marine Corp. He served a four-year stint and then moved back to California.

Ken was hired as a cop in St. Helena in 1936. Only a year after pinning on the badge, Ken married Beverly Street, a fellow transplant to the city. Ken and Beverly formed a loving family when daughters Patricia and Kennie joined them. In 1944, Ken was drafted back into the military, this time the U.S. Army. He was assigned to an airborne artillery unit and took part in the campaign to retake the Philippines under the direction of General Douglas McArthur. After the war, Ken returned to St. Helena, only to be promptly recruited by then Calistoga police chief Ed Light to take his spot. Ken moved his young family ten minutes up the road to Calistoga and never left.

Ken cared deeply for his adopted home of Calistoga. He organized a yearly tradition of police officers collecting toys and food baskets for

Above: Calistoga police chief Ken Hively wore this style of shoulder patch during this career. *Courtesy of the Napa Police Historical Society.*

Ken poses with his patrol car in 1947. *Courtesy of the Napa Police Historical Society.*

underprivileged families, and then Santa and his helper officers would distribute them.

Ken's love of sports became evident when, in 1955, the most famous boxer of his era, Rocky Marciano, came to Calistoga to train for an upcoming defense of his World Heavyweight title in nearby San Francisco. Ken was the president of the local chamber of commerce at the time, so undoubtedly, that played into his feelings. He lobbied hard for Rocky to make Calistoga his base. Ken and the entire town of Calistoga got swept up in the excitement. The town shut down for the day, and a parade was held. Two local bar owners of Italian descent tacked a homemade banner up on the local theater marque, announcing, "To Your Health, Rocky" in Italian. The town's two fire engines led the way, with Rocky riding in a convertible. The town threw a welcome banquet for Rocky, and he was named both honorary police chief and mayor.

From that day forward, for the next few months, Ken and five of his officers, basically the whole force, provided around-the-clock security for Rocky and his entourage as they trained at the Calistoga Fairgrounds and stayed at a local motel. Ken became so close to Rocky that when the title fight happened in San Francisco's Kezar Stadium, Ken was chosen to be one of the people in Rocky's corner. Calistoga's love affair with Rocky was evident in the custom silk boxing robe they presented to him; it had the logo "Rocky Marciano—Calistoga's Adopted Son."

In December 1958, the sleepy town of Calistoga was jilted awake when a would-be bank robber got more than he bargained for. Robert Gladu was a down-on-his-luck, unemployed janitor in Marin County. Faced with an overdrawn bank account and the desire to buy Christmas presents for a lady friend and her children, Gladu did what any reasonable person would do: he robbed a bank. The robbery in the small Marin town of Fairfax netted Gladu $910 by simply handing the teller a threating note. Emboldened by his success, Gladu decided the Bank of America in Calistoga was ripe for the picking. He didn't account for bank manager Frank Piner, who was a special police officer, or Calistoga's top cop, Ken.

Gladu strode into the bank in Calistoga, went directly to a women teller, handed her a note that stated, "Desperate and trigger-happy" and demanded $785. The shaking teller gave Gladu the money, and he strode out. Piner and another teller were oblivious until after Gladu left. Finally alerted to the heist, Piner grabbed the phone and dialed the police station, but he got a busy signal. He grabbed his .32-caliber semiautomatic pistol and ran out after the robber. Unfortunately for Gladu, he wasn't a local,

Professional boxer Rocky Marciano and Ken share a candid moment during a break in Rocky's training regime. *Courtesy of the Napa Police Historical Society.*

so he didn't know that the stretch of Washington Street he was driving on was a dead-end street that only exited near the Southern Pacific Railroad Station. In the meantime, Piner pulled a move straight out of an action film: he commandeered a car driving by and ordered the driver to head for the railroad station, keen to the fact that there was only one exit. Stymied by the road, Gladu made a U-turn and found Piner standing in the middle of the road pointing a pistol at him. Gladu got out of his car and quickly gave up. Piner and a male teller who had run over to help marched Gladu back to the bank, where the remaining tellers were waiting for the police who they thought Piner had called, not knowing about the busy signal. Ken was finally alerted and ran over to the bank to slap the cuffs on Gladu. At the time, the local paper reported this was Calistoga's first bank robbery in recorded history.

Ken hung up his holster in 1971. He stayed on, serving as the city's police commissioner for another four years. In this role, he advised the town council on all matters related to the police department and its budget.

In a fitting nod to Calistoga's reputation for its hot springs and health resorts, Ken had a second career after retirement as a masseur at the Calistoga Spa Hot Springs Resort. The Hot Springs Resort was one of the many spas in town that catered to the steady flow of Bay Area residents looking to rest and rejuvenate. Ken suffered a massive heart attack at his Calistoga home in early 1978; he was rushed to the nearby St. Helena Hospital but didn't survive.

11

DELPH REXROTH

Delph "Rex" Rexroth was born in Wyoming in 1909 and was raised in Nebraska. Like many children of the Great Depression, Rex learned to make his own way early in life, holding a variety of odd jobs starting at the young age of eleven years old. He later described himself as a jack of all trades and called himself a truck driver, car salesman, breaker of horses and cat skinner, all before the age of twenty-one. Rex married his high school sweetheart in 1927. Together they had three children.

Rex was drawn to Napa because of tragedy. In 1936, his father, who was the caretaker of a property near the Napa/Sonoma county line, passed away unexpectedly. Rex moved his family to California to help care for his mother. He took a job driving a milk truck and later a cement mixer to make ends meet.

Tragically, death followed Rex to California, when his wife passed away unexpectedly in 1937. He met and married his second wife, Harriet, two years later, in 1939.

Above: The first and only inspector of police badge issued by the Napa Police Department. The title of inspector was retired when Delph Rexroth did. *Courtesy of the Napa Police Historical Society.*

Rex's first foray into Napa law enforcement came in 1940 as a special police officer; these were akin to the modern reserve officers, brought on for limited duty when there was a major event or natural disaster. His full-time job was as a postal worker.

When World War II broke out, Rex went to work for the Napa Sheriff's Department as a part-time deputy. His assignment was to fulfill a request from the U.S. Treasury Department to fingerprint all resident aliens in the Napa County. Napa County had a large migrant population, including large contingents of Italians, Chinese and Mexicans. By the time he was done, he had personally fingerprinted about 5,000 people, including 1,200 mental patients at the Napa State Hospital.

Rex's hard work did not go unnoticed, and Sheriff John Claussen appointed him as a full-time deputy when a spot opened in 1942. He was one of four sworn members of the department and made a whopping $150 a month. Just as the war was ending, Rex made the move to the Napa Police Department. He was enticed by two carrots: a $25 a month pay raise and the promise of being named an inspector. Rex got the money but would have to wait seven years to attain the title of inspector.

Throughout the history of law enforcement in Napa County, it has been common for cops to move between departments. In fact, four of Napa County's sheriffs started as police officers at the Napa Police Department before being elected as Napa's County's top cop (John Claussen, Earl Randol, Gary Simpson and Doug Koford). There has always been a close working and social relationship among officers in the county's various departments. One tangible expression of this was the Napa County Peace Officers Association (NCPOA). It was founded as a pistol shooting club in 1949, with its ranks made of officers from every department in the county. Later, the group morphed into a social club of sorts and offered scholarships for college students interested in criminal justice and a bereavement benefit for the loved ones of officers who passed away. Each year, the NCPOA would host a Peace Officers Ball. The ball was the place to see and be seen in Napa. In its heyday, it featured full orchestras, lavish dinners and plenty of booze.

When Sherwood Munk took over as the chief in 1952, one of his first acts was to appoint Rex as an inspector. As Inspector Rexroth, he was in charge of sending criminal complaints to the district attorney's office, preparing reports for court, making sure witnesses showed up to court, walking prisoners between the jail and courthouse and serving as the bailiff during Napa police–related trials.

Opposite: Rex poses next to his police car in 1949. An auxiliary forward-facing red light can be seen mounted to the car's front fender. During this era, the patrol cars didn't have overhead emergency lights mounted on the roof, and rotating lights weren't widely in use; instead, officers relied on these easier-to-install spotlights. *Courtesy of the Napa Police Historical Society.*

Above: Officer Chuck Holden and Rex pose with a poster advertising the 1960 Peace Officers Ball, an annual tradition hosted by the Napa County Peace Officers Association. *Courtesy of the Napa Police Historical Society.*

Right: A smiling Rex poses in the early 1950s. His rank of inspector can be seen on his hat piece. *Courtesy of the Napa Police Historical Society.*

Rex and his wife, Harriet, are all smiles at his retirement party, held in 1964. Rex is holding a gold-and-silver Western-style belt buckle with a badge logo at the center—a fitting retirement gift for the avid horseman. *Courtesy of the Napa Police Historical Society.*

Tragedy struck the Rexroth family in 1957, when Richard, Rex's oldest son, died in one of the worst traffic collisions in the county's history. Richard and four others lost their lives. Richard had survived the horrors of the Korean War and was only twenty-two years old when he died.

As it turned out, Rex was the one and only inspector that the Napa Police Department ever had. The position was retired with him in 1964, and his duties were split between several junior officers on a rotating basis.

Rex was an avid horseman; he belonged to the Napa Valley Horseman's Association and served on the group's board. Rex also volunteered his time as a member of the Napa County Mounted Posse. The all-volunteer posse is a group administered by the Napa County Sheriff's Department that helps with search-and-rescue operations in the rural areas of the county and participates in parades and other ceremonial functions. Napa's Mounted Posse is one of the longest serving in California.

When the local newspaper asked Rex whether he'd become a lawman all over again, his answer was blunt and to the point: "Rexroth said if he had it to do over again he would choose law enforcement work as it was when he went into it. But as it is today, he isn't sure. The pay is low for the risk you take and the amount of work you do, he commented, and most serious of all, he said, 'it seems that every law made today is for the benefit of the law violator rather than the officers.'"

In retirement, Rex could be seen riding his beloved John Deere tractor, tending to his two-acre parcel on the west side of town, on Laurel Street in the Westwood neighborhood. The area has since been subdivided into tract homes. Rex passed away in 1981.

12

CHUCK HANSEN

Charles "Chuck" Hansen was born in Davenport, Iowa, in 1926. His family moved to the Solano County town of Benicia, where Chuck excelled in sports. Chuck held several jobs before becoming a Napa police officer, including at the nearby Benicia Arsenal, the U.S. Army's largest ordnance depot on the West Coast. When asked later why he chose a career in law enforcement, Chuck said, "I was in search of something I wouldn't get laid off of." Chuck started as a parking enforcement officer, writing tickets in the downtown area for ten months until a police officer position opened. He was sworn in as a police officer in 1954.

Chuck recalled his early days on the force during a feature article in the *Napa Register* newspaper: "Hansen remembers stopping an angry motorist in the early morning hours near Napa High School. Each of the other two cops on duty that night had already pulled him over. 'I told him not to worry,' said Hansen. 'I'm the last officer in town and the city limits is a block away.'"

Above: Chuck Hansen's trusty Crown Graflex camera shot four-by-five-inch negatives. He had a developing studio in the basement of the police station. This camera documented many scenes of horror and destruction before it was donated to the Napa Police Historical Society by the department in 2009. By that time, print photography had already been replaced by digital. *Courtesy of the Napa Police Historical Society.*

Chuck holds a sixteen-gauge shotgun that he found in the car of David Lyle Smith, who shot his ex-wife. She survived, and Smith was charged with attempted murder. Chuck noted that the shotgun had one discharged shell and two unused shells. *Courtesy of the Napa Police Historical Society.*

Chuck spent seventeen of his twenty-nine years on the force in the Investigations Bureau. He was one of the first full-time detectives at the department. Before the 1960s, any in-depth investigative work was handled by the chief of police or his assistant. As the number of serious crimes increased, the department chose to employ trained detectives whose sole job was to investigate the most serious crimes. Chuck started as a detective but rapidly became known for his keen eye with a camera and meticulous documentation of crime scenes.

Chuck pioneered the field of forensic sciences at the Napa Police Department. Before the 1960s, if there was a major crime scene or traffic accident, the department called the *Napa Register* and asked its crime beat photographer, Bob McKenzie, to document the scene. In 2009, Bob's widow donated his photographic negative collection related to public safety topics to the Napa Police Historical Society. The collection included many graphic photographs of murders, suicides and fatal traffic accidents, all of which attest to the mutually beneficial relationship he shared with the department.

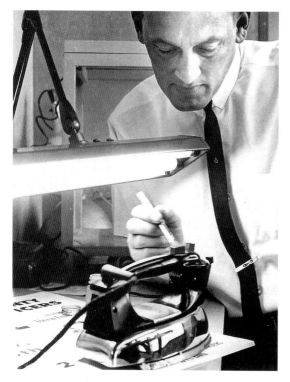

Chuck fingerprints an iron used during the bludgeoning murder of a young woman in 1965. The blood and fingerprints collected were important during the investigation of the case, which eventually led to the murderer turning himself in and pleading guilty to second-degree murder. *Courtesy of the Napa Police Historical Society.*

Indeed, many retired officers from this era have very nice reprints of photographs that included them engaged in police work. McKenzie made it a point to provide copies of photographs published in the newspaper to the officers—a smart way to keep on good terms with the cops.

Arguably the most famous crime scene Chuck documented with his Graflex camera was the 1974 murder of Anita Andrews at Fagiani's Bar in downtown Napa. Anita Andrews was the daughter of the bar's founder, and she and her sister, Muriel, inherited the bar when their father died. Muriel found Anita's body in the back room of the bar after Anita failed to show up for her day job at the Napa State Hospital. Chuck collected the evidence that would become key to finally solving the case thirty-seven years later—discarded cigarette butts in one of the bar's ashtrays. The use of DNA to identify criminals was still two decades away, yet Chuck's meticulous scene processing would pay off.

In 2010, Napa police detectives sent off some of the evidence Chuck collected to take advantage of the advances made in DNA extraction and testing. A male DNA profile was extracted from the cigarette butts and bloody rag Chuck had preserved, catalogued and stored away in the

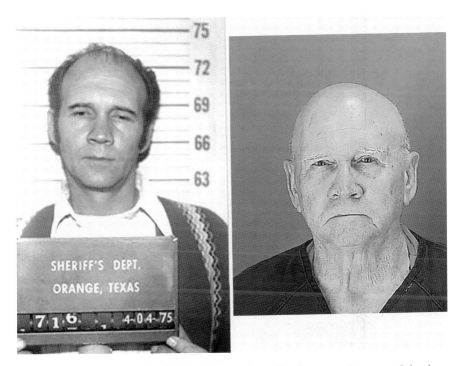

Serial killer Roy Melanson in side-by-side mug shots. The first was taken around the time Napa's Anita Andrews was killed in 1976 and the second when he went to trial in Napa in 2011. *Courtesy of the Orange County (Texas) Sheriff's Department and Napa County Department of Corrections.*

evidence vault all those years before. That profile didn't match any of the prime suspects who Napa detectives had investigated over the intervening decades. It turned out to match a man named Roy Melanson, a person totally unknown to Napa detectives and thus completely off the radar. Melanson was a career criminal who was already serving a life sentence in a Colorado prison for the murder of a young woman in 1974, a crime that happened just two months after Andrews was killed in Napa. Melanson's DNA was collected and uploaded to the nationwide database after his Colorado conviction in 1992, leading to the hit with Napa's unknown profile in the system. This case would never have been solved without the crucial evidence collected by Chuck. Melanson had no ties to Napa—he was a drifter who blew through town, committed the murder and was gone the next day. Melanson was later tied to two other unsolved cold case murders of young women, one in Texas and another in Louisiana. Unquestionably, there were other victims of Melanson, as he crisscrossed the country for decades.

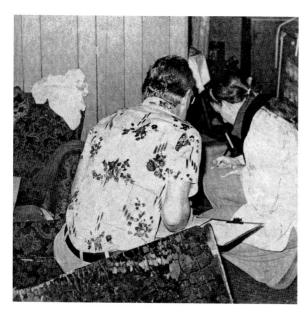

One of the last major crime scenes that Chuck processed was the still-unsolved axe murder of a man in 1980. The killer attempted to cover their tracks by setting the victim's home ablaze. Chuck can be seen here working with his hand-picked successor, Janet York (Lipsey). *Courtesy of the Napa Police Historical Society.*

Melanson was extradited to Napa from Colorado and finally went to trial in 2011. He was a shadow of the young drifter who preyed on vulnerable women; Melanson was elderly and confined to a wheelchair. He was convicted of first-degree murder and promptly returned to his jail cell in a Colorado prison to serve out his lengthy sentence there, with an invitation to come back to a California prison if ever released there.

Chuck was the first and last sworn police officer to hold the title of crime scene investigator. He trained his hand-picked successor, civilian employee Janet York (Lipsey) starting in 1980. From that time forward, a civilian would serve as the department's primary crime scene investigator, yet a small cadre of specially trained police officers would continue to investigate crime scenes, serving in an ancillary capacity when needed.

Chuck retired as a detective sergeant in 1983. He passed away in 2006 after a long battle with dementia.

13

CHUCK HOLDEN

C harles "Chuck" Holden was a native of Iowa. His first job as an adult was as an attendant at a mental hospital in Woodward, Iowa. Chuck enlisted in the navy during World War II and was first exposed the Napa area during this time. He served at the Mare Island Naval Shipyard, in the nearby city of Vallejo, in the neuropsychological wing of the naval hospital. He tended to soldiers who returned from war with scars that couldn't be seen, dealing with post-traumatic stress disorder before the term was created. At the time, they called it "battle fatigue" or "shell shock." After the war was over, he started his civilian law enforcement career by serving as a traffic officer at Mare Island and then moved to Napa to take a job at the Napa Ice Company.

Chuck was larger than life. He and several other officers hired during the 1950s met the most important qualification: they were big burly men who could take care of themselves in a fight. Chuck and his friend Clint Forloine were both hired away from the ice company, another job that required brawn (picture manhandling large blocks of ice). They both had long careers as police officers, and Clint retired as a captain.

Above: This intricately engraved belt buckle includes the retirement badge that was presented to Chuck Holden in 1985. *Courtesy of the Napa Police Historical Society.*

Chuck investigates a commercial burglary in this undated photograph. *Courtesy of the Napa Police Historical Society.*

Chuck was known as one of the early adopters of the Junior Traffic Safety Patrol (JTSP) in Napa. The JTSP was first created by American Automobile Association in 1920 as a program to teach elementary school children traffic safety and use them as crossing guards at their own schools; it spread nationwide. The program was brought to Napa by the Napa Police Department in the early 1950s, when Officer Earl Randol pitched the idea to then chief Sherwood Munk. Chuck served alongside Earl as an advisor to several of the schools that participated in the program, and Chuck would eventually take over the whole Napa program, spearheading it during the 1970s and '80s. Retired Napa Superior Court judge (and Napa native) Ray Guadagni fondly recalled his years in the JTSP and gave high praise to Chuck and his fellow officer advisor/coaches in his 2016 memoir, stating, "Special thanks must be given to those officers who coached our patrol kids. The good look of the patrol and the precision of their movements were vital to drawing the attention and respect of both drivers and students crossing the street. The high quality of Napa's patrol were a testament to not only the patrol students, but also to their coaches."

When I conducted an oral history interview with Chuck in 2006, he waxed nostalgic while remembering his time leading the Traffic Safety Patrol. Chuck, who was in his eighties at the time, broke out a bottle of

Left: This uniform hat was worn by members of Napa's Junior Traffic Safety Patrol. The program was sponsored by the American Automobile Association (AAA). *Courtesy of the Napa Police Historical Society.*

Right: This is the first patch worn by Napa's Junior Traffic Safety Patrol. It features the initials NJTP (Napa Junior Traffic Patrol). It was during this time that Chuck began working as a mentor in the program. *Courtesy of the Napa Police Historical Society.*

whiskey and regaled me with stories of how each year the Traffic Safety Patrol's efforts culminated in a ceremony at Napa's Memorial Stadium. Each elementary school's team would march in, and awards would be given to students for various achievements in the patrol. Chuck also led the popular and fun Simon Says activity during the ceremony. Chuck excused himself in the middle of our interview, rummaged around in a cabinet and produced a stack of photographs. While he was in each, the focus was not him, it was the students he mentored in the Traffic Safety Patrol. The photographs were groups shots of various elementary school patrols, all dating from the 1970s. The pride in Chuck's face that afternoon spoke volumes about the impact that the JTSP had—not only on the students.

In my time as a cop in Napa, I frequently encounter lifelong Napa residents. Many of them have told me their first interaction with law enforcement was while serving as an "officer" in the Traffic Safety Patrol. To a person, they have fond memories of Chuck and his fellow officers

Chuck and an unidentified member of the Junior Traffic Safety Patrol pose outside a local school. *Courtesy of the Napa Police Historical Society.*

who drilled them on marching and ensured they were safe while carrying out their duties as crossing guards.

In addition to the Junior Traffic Safety Patrol, Chuck supervised two other specialized units in the department: he was the officer liaison for the reserve police officer program and led the traffic unit.

Above: Chuck poses with members of the traffic unit in 1983. Chuck supervised the traffic unit for the last few years of his career. Seen on their Honda motorcycles are (*left to right*): Jim Cody, Gary Schager and Chuck Holden. *Courtesy of the Napa Police Historical Society.*

Left: This portrait of Chuck was made the year he retired, 1983. Visible are hash marks on the left sleeve of Chuck's shirt; each mark represents five years of service. *Courtesy of the Napa Police Historical Society.*

The Reserve Police Officer program was an enhancement of the long practice of hiring special officers to help when the regular force needed it. The unpaid reserve officers wore similar uniforms as regular officers and were armed. Many times they worked in tandem with full-time officers. Other times they conducted checks of homes for citizens who were on vacation or participated in community outreach events. Chuck's job was to provide the reserves with ongoing training, perform inspections of their uniforms and equipment and schedule them for work shifts.

The traffic unit has been around since Officer Ed Glos started patrolling on his Harley in the 1930s. The unit has fluctuated from two to six officers assigned to motorcycles, depending on the priorities and budgets at the police department. Chuck was a longtime motorcycle rider and a natural fit to supervise the unit. The unit was responsible for enforcing traffic laws and investigating major traffic collisions.

When Chuck retired in 1985, he stayed active. He ran a successful farm tractor rental business, tilling farm fields in the area. Chuck was also an active member of the Napa County Peace Officers Association, a fraternal group made of officers from various agencies in the county that started in the 1940s. He served as the group's treasurer for more than a decade.

Chuck passed away peacefully at home in 2010 after a brief illness. Before he passed, Chuck donated his extensive collection of Traffic Safety Patrol photographs and memorabilia to the Napa Police Historical Society.

KEN NARLOW

Kenneth Allen Narlow was born in Wisconsin in 1930. Ken knew early on that he wanted to be a cop but deferred that dream to serve his country in the military, joining the navy at seventeen. He received training in intelligence and was posted to Skaggs Island, a satellite base of the Mare Island Naval Shipyard in Vallejo. While stationed at Skaggs Island, Ken met his future wife, Marie, a Napa resident. When Ken was discharged from the navy, he had trouble finding a full-time job. He went back to the military, this time serving in the air force for eight years. Ken and Marie decided to settle down in Napa and start his long-planned law enforcement career. They bought a newly built house in the Northwood neighborhood. In 1959, he applied to become a Napa County sheriff's deputy. About one hundred people applied, and Ken ranked number four on the list after testing. The sheriff hired the top four candidates; thus, Ken started his career serving Napa. He later reflected on his decision, saying, "It was a good job. Steady pay."

Like all rookie cops, Ken did his time driving a patrol car. He spent the first four years in uniform patrolling the Napa Valley, mostly on the graveyard shift. During those early years, there was only one deputy working the graveyard

Above: Captain Ken Narlow's retirement badge, presented to him in 1987. *Courtesy of the Napa Police Historical Society.*

In 1961, Napa sheriff's deputies Bill Bishop and Ken Narlow pose in their state patrol costumes during a break while filming the Elvis Presley movie *Wild in the Country*. *Courtesy of the Napa Police Historical Society.*

shift. If Ken needed help, he'd radio for one of the city police officers (Napa, St. Helena or Calistoga) or a California Highway Patrol officer to lend a hand.

In 1961, Ken had only been on the job for two years. He and his friend fellow deputy Bill Bishop landed smack-dab in the middle of the biggest thing to happen in Napa County that year: Elvis. Ken and Bill were tapped to be extras during the filming of *Wild in the Country*, which was doing location filming in the Napa Valley. Ken and Bill played state troopers. In fact, they were pressed into real duty one day when the cast and crew was filming on location near the busy Silverado Trail. Traffic was jammed by drivers trying to catch a glimpse of the King. Ken and

Ken as he appeared in 1969, the year he began investigating the Zodiac serial murder case. *Courtesy of the Napa Police Historical Society.*

Bill sprang into action, directing traffic on the roadway, dressed in their fictional state trooper costumes. Ken received an autographed photo from Elvis, which still hangs proudly in the family home.

Ken then took a job as a detective and never left the unit. He had found his passion and excelled at teasing out the clues and solving complex crimes. He took a promotion to sergeant of the unit. His next natural step would have been a promotion to lieutenant, and Ken took the test. He had second thoughts about leaving the job he loved and pulled his name from consideration. As luck would have it, the sheriff tapped Ken to fill an unexpected vacancy as captain of the detective unit when someone was terminated. No matter what his rank, Ken never stopped pitching in when needed.

Although the most famous case Ken worked on was the still-unsolved Zodiac murders in 1969, it would be a mistake to pigeonhole him as the "Zodiac detective." Unfortunately, if you search Ken's name on Google, that is all you will find. His name and photograph are featured on various Zodiac enthusiast websites. By his own count, Ken worked on over seventy homicide cases. He was part of a small team of dedicated detectives at the sheriff's department; partnered with John Robertson and Dick Lonergan, these men worked on every homicide case in the unincorporated areas of the county during the 1960s through 1980s.

Ken posed for this photograph in 1987, to be used in the newspaper article announcing his retirement. *Courtesy of the Napa Police Historical Society.*

In 1986, Ken decided to make a run for sheriff. The post had been vacated by the untimely death of Sheriff Philip "Bucky" Stewart, who died of a heart attack. Ken garnered the most votes in the primary but lost a close election to then Napa police sergeant Gary Simpson. Ken retired as a captain in 1987, after a twenty-eight-year career. Coworkers who spent years working side by side with Ken heaped praise on him. Dick Lonergan said, "If you were to describe a great investigator who cared about his cases and cared about doing a really professional job, you'd have to print Ken's picture."

Ken worked during retirement for a travel agency for a time and then drove a school bus for the Napa Valley Unified School District. When Ken found out that he didn't have enough seniority to drive the away buses that took sports teams to their games, he switched to driving for Justin-Siena Catholic High School. He excelled at the job and was promoted to director of transportation for the school. Ken was lured away by a job that put his detective skills to work again: working as a check fraud investigator for Vallergas, a local grocery chain. Yet even in retirement, Ken was still associated with the Zodiac murder case. Even three decades later, Ken received letters from amateur sleuths and self-taught code breakers who were convinced they had uncovered the "real" killer. Ken was gracious, even with the most outlandish and obsessed people. He was quick to steer them to whichever detective at the sheriff's department was assigned the case at the time.

In 2007, Ken was approached by a production company that was mounting a feature movie based on author Robert Graysmith's best-selling novel *Zodiac*. Ken was brought on as a consultant for the film. Retired deputy Dave Collins, the first deputy on scene at the Napa County murder scene, was also brought on to help. The director strove for reality in the re-creations of the Zodiac murders in the film. When it came time to re-create the killing that happened in Napa County, at the recreation area of Lake Berryessa, the production company found that the spit of land where the attack happened had changed since 1969; the cluster of oak trees at the site had been removed years before. The producers paid for fully grown replacements to be helicoptered in and transplanted. The production company also brought Ken face-to-face with the surviving victim from the Lake Berryessa attack, Bryan Hartnell. It was the first time Ken had seen Hartnell since 1969.

Ken was proud of his work on the film. He paid out of his own pocket to charter a tour bus and invited fifty of his family, friends and former coworkers to accompany him to the film's Northern California opening at the Metreon Theater in San Francisco.

In 2010, Ken lost a long battle with cancer.

15

HAROLD SNOOK

Harold "Hal" Snook was an unassuming man, small in stature, yet he had a large impact on the Napa County Sheriff's Department. Hal was born in 1925 in the hamlet of Capella in Mendocino County. His family moved to the nearby town of Ukiah, where Hal developed a love of journalism. He was so interested that while in high school he took a part-time job as a reporter for the local newspaper. Hal's career plans were interrupted like so many other young men when the United States entered World War II. Hal enlisted in the U.S. Army and was part of the island-hopping campaign in the South Pacific.

Hal returned from war and went off to college at San Jose State College, where he obtained a journalism degree and married his wife, Barbara. He worked as editor of the *Western Sentinel* in the tiny Siskiyou County town of

Above: Hal Snook's frequent companion during crime scene processing was his trusty tobacco pipe. One of these pipes is pictured here, along with his deputy sheriff badge. *Courtesy of Larry Snook.*

Etna. Hal and Barbara moved to the "big city" of Napa in 1951, when he took over as the editor of the *Napa Journal*, a weekly newspaper. War once again interrupted Hal's plans, when he was called back to service in 1951, during the Korean War.

Hal served three years as an air force officer during the Korean War. It was during this time that Hal developed an interest in law enforcement. He was assigned to a security police detachment while deployed to the Korean peninsula enforcing military law on the deployed servicemen.

Hal's other love besides journalism was being an outdoorsman. He was an avid hunter and fisherman. After he got out of the air force, he turned these loves into a career by opening a sporting goods store in Napa.

In 1961, Hal joined the Napa Police Department as a dispatcher, becoming one of the first full-time dispatchers employed by the department. A year later, he became a deputy at the Napa County Sheriff's Department.

Hal landed a job as a detective in 1967 and was first assigned to combat the burgeoning drug problem that was plaguing Napa County (and the rest of the country). This was the era of hippies and free love, and narcotics became more common in the form of marijuana, psilocybin mushrooms, heroin and LSD. Eventually, the sheriffs would team with other agencies in the county to form the Napa Special Investigations Bureau (NSIB). It was from Hal's position as a detective that he launched his career as a crime scene investigator and created the sheriff's department's crime laboratory from scratch. He was recognized by the U.S. Supreme Court as an expert in narcotics and fingerprint identification. He also taught crime scene investigation classes at the Napa Valley Community College for many years.

When Hal was set to retire, he was interviewed by the *Napa Register* newspaper. The one case that he said he was most proud of working on was the Willy the Woodcutter case in 1971. Pacific Union College (PUC) is a Seventh-day Adventist school. PUC coed Lynda Kanes disappeared while driving to work. Her vehicle was later located on the side of Howell Mountain Road, one of the main roadways that lead from the valley floor to campus. Over five hundred students from PUC volunteered to help deputies in the intensive search of the area. In the end, two deputies located Kanes's body about two hundred yards from the roadway, partially buried in a pile of rocks and leaves. Her head was covered by a cut portion of a U.S. Army duffle bag and wrapped in a torn and tattered forty-eight-star U.S. flag. A gas can was near the body, and the smell of gas was noted on her body, possibly indicating the suspect had planned to cover up the crime further. An autopsy would later reveal that she died of blunt force trauma to her head.

Left: In this undated photograph, Hal uses a specialized camera to capture an image from a school yearbook for use later in a photographic lineup. Hal is smoking one of his signature pipes. *Courtesy of the Napa Police Historical Society.*

Below: In this 1969 photograph, Hal kneels and points to a tire tread he found that possibly belonged to the Zodiac serial killer's vehicle. The VW Karmann Ghia visible at the left of the photograph was owned by one of the Zodiac's victims, Bryan Hartnell. *Courtesy of the Napa Police Historical Society.*

(FX4)NAPA, Calif., July 23--CONVICTED SLAYER LEAVES COURT--Walter Boyd
Williams, 57, leaves court at Napa today following his conviction of
first degree murder in the Feb. 26 slaying of Pacific Union College
coed Lynda Kanes, 20. With the St. Helena, Calif., woodcutter, is
Napa County Sheriff's Capt. Bill Bishop.(AP Wirephoto)(sjv61600napa)
1971

This *Napa Register* newspaper photograph was picked up and reprinted across the country by the Associated Press. It shows Walter Williams, better known as Willie the Woodcutter, after his first-degree murder conviction. Williams is followed out of the courtroom by Napa County sheriff's captain Bill Bishop. *Courtesy of the Associated Press.*

Fifty-seven-year-old Walter Boyd Williams resided in a small cottage with his wife and four children at the intersection of Silverado Trail and Howell Mountain Road, about three miles from where Lynda's body had been found. He ran a woodcutting business and was known by locals as Willie the Woodcutter. Hal and his fellow detectives checked on known sex offenders who lived in the area, and Walter had been accused of a rape in the 1950s, so he was on their radar. Other coeds from PUC also told detectives that Walter would sometimes wave at them as they drove by his house and that Lynda had talked to Walter in passing on several occasions. They obtained a search warrant for Walter's property and to collect biological samples from him, as well gas cans and trace evidence. The evidence collected would become key later.

The case hinged in large part on the forensic evidence, and Hal was a key player in collecting and preserving that evidence. He worked jointly with

Peter Barnett, a private crime scene consultant based in the Berkeley who consulted on many high-profile murders around the Bay Area.

The two keystones of any forensic examination are collection and preservation of evidence at the scene of the crime (and from the victim's body) and collection and preservation of evidence from the suspect to link him/her to the crime. Hal and Peter put on a master class in forensics in this case.

Red fibers from the flag found with Lynda matched red fibers located just outside the front door of Walter's house. The duffle bag that held Lynda's body contained paint chips that matched chips located in the laundry room of Wayne's house. A few minute hair fragments located on Lynda's body were consistent with Walter's pubic hair samples collected by Hal and Peter. After a lengthy trial, Walter was convicted of first-degree murder and sentenced to life in prison.

Hal retired in May 1980 and opened a jewelry and fossil business and was a member of the Napa Rock & Gem Club. Hal and his wife cut the stones and did custom metalwork on the jewelry they sold. They also dug and prepared fossil fish from Wyoming and sold them to museums, dealers and collectors worldwide. Hal passed away in 2010.

16

RICHARD LONERGAN

Richard "Dick" Lonergan's family has been in the Napa Valley for over 150 years. His great-grandfather John Lonergan emigrated from Ireland and settled in Napa in 1865. He purchased a ranch in the Coombsville area on the east side of Napa, where he and his wife, Margaret, raised their three sons.

In an ironic twist, John Lonergan almost met an untimely death in 1863, which would have spelled the end of the Lonergan family line. John was walking to his home from downtown Napa when he was set upon by Charley and Dan English, brothers in crime from a notorious Napa family. The English brothers tried to rob John of a fifty-dollar gold piece. John made a run for it and jumped into the Napa River as one of the brothers shot at him, luckily missing. The Lonergan clan would later produce two long-serving Napa lawmen, Dick at the Napa County Sheriff's Department and his brother Dan, who worked at the Napa Police Department.

Dick attended Napa High School, where he graduated in 1958. In addition to being a stand-out athlete, Dick was also the student body president both his junior and senior years. He became known by the nickname "Mr. Napa."

Above: This undersheriff badge was the last one worn by Richard "Dick" Lonergan during his long and storied career at the Napa County Sheriff's Department. *Courtesy of the Napa Police Historical Society.*

Dick with fellow Napa County sheriff's deputies in this undated photograph from the 1950s. Dick is at the far left. *Courtesy of the Napa Police Historical Society.*

He excelled in sports, student government and academics at Napa High. Although Dick's first love was football, he also excelled in track and field, swimming and basketball, earning him the title of Athlete of the Year in 1958. Later in life, he was inducted into the Napa High School Hall of Fame. He served in the U.S. Navy right out of high school and then decided to pursue his interest in law enforcement.

In 1963, after completing his service in the U.S. Navy, Dick joined the Napa Sheriff's Department. He worked his way up the ranks, and by 1969, he was a sergeant, serving in the detective bureau, where he was heavily involved in the investigation of the infamous Zodiac murder case. At that same time, he worked on a lesser-known case that framed his excellence as a detective.

Less than three weeks after the Zodiac killer brutally attacked a young couple at Lake Berryessa, a new case emerged involving a young teenager. Nancy Breiling was fifteen years old and a sophomore at Armijo High School. On this particular day, she had been volunteering to care for

The grave site of Nancy Breitling, whose life was tragically cut short in 1969. *Courtesy of the Napa Police Historical Society.*

young children in the child development center at the Church of Latter-day Saints in Fairfield, California. That day was like the others, and at about 4:00 p.m., she started the familiar two-mile walk back to her home. This was a routine walk that she had made many times, but this time she didn't make it home. Her mother, Gloria, became worried when Nancy wasn't home for the family's normal 6:00 p.m. dinner. Nancy was always very punctual, so shortly after 6:00 p.m., Gloria reported her daughter missing to the Fairfield Police Department. She told officers how reliable Nancy was and that the family had agreed-on routes that the children could walk between the house and various locations, such as church and downtown. Fairfield Police searched the area where Nancy was last seen but found nothing.

The next day, on a rural roadway in Wooden Valley, about ten miles away from where Nancy was last seen, a motorist made a horrific discovery. This passing motorist found Nancy's lifeless body just before noon. Wooden Valley Road is an area that straddles the counties of Napa and Solano, so the first call went to the California Highway Patrol, which quickly called in the Solano County Sheriff's Department. The CHP and Solano sheriff determined that the crime scene was about a half mile inside Napa County, so Dick and the Napa County sheriffs were also called. The body was fully clothed, except for one shoe and a sock that was found knotted around Nancy's neck. That very sock and was used to take her life. Detectives combed the area for clues and found Nancy's purse and her missing shoe discarded in different spots along the roadway, about a tenth of a mile from

Dick stops for a quick photograph inside the Napa County Sheriff's Department in 1988. By this time, he held the rank of captain in the department. *Courtesy of the Napa Police Historical Society.*

her body. Dick theorized that the killer had thrown the items out of his car as he drove off, getting rid of the last items he thought could connect him to the grisly crime.

Suspicion initially fell on the Zodiac killer, since Nancy's body was found within miles of his last attack—and surely because this name was on everyone's lips. As Dick delved into Nancy's crime scene, he quickly ruled it out as a Zodiac killing. First, there was no letter from the Zodiac taunting authorities, which were mailed without fail after each of his murders. Secondly, the autopsy revealed that Nancy had been strangled, which didn't fit the pattern of Zodiac murders. Lastly, Nancy didn't fit the profile of a Zodiac victim, who to that point had been young adult couples attacked at remote yet well-known spots for couples to park.

Dick, John Robertson and their fellow detectives embarked on a key step in any murder investigation: tracing the victim's movements in the days or hours before the crime. In this case, there had already been a missing persons case filed with the Fairfield Police by her parents. They interviewed the last people to see Nancy alive and delved into her normal daily activities.

Darrell Dean Meneley was a twenty-two-year-old Napan who had been in the headlines three weeks before the murder for his heroic efforts saving the lives of three young children. After happening on a house fully engulfed in flames, Meneley ran in and pulled the three children from the burning home. Meneley was the youngest of eleven children and a former patient at the iconic Napa State Mental Hospital. While enrolled at the local community college, he took a job working for a Napa laundry service, where he drove a delivery truck every day between Napa and Fairfield. He drove a white panel truck—the same type that a key witness saw parked on the shoulder of the Wooden Valley Road around the time that Nancy was killed. The witness recalled a distinctive primer spot on one of the truck's fenders.

Dick and his fellow detectives went to the laundry company where Meneley worked. They learned that Meneley returned over four hours

Detectives examine the body of Richard Niemeier at the scene of his 1979 murder. Dick is standing at the far right next to fellow detective John Robertson, who is pointing. Seen at the far left, wearing a leather jacket, is crime scene investigator Hal Snook. *Courtesy of the Napa Police Historical Society.*

late from his normal routine and that one of Meneley's coworkers found a pair of women's prescription glasses in Meneley's delivery truck on the night of the murder. Meneley told the coworker that the glasses belonged to his wife; however, trial testimony by a Fairfield optometrist would later link them to Nancy.

This case was focused on forensic evidence. Peter Barnett, a criminalist based in Berkeley who helped on many Napa cases of this era, found a blood stain on Meneley's shirt that matched Nancy's blood type. Using a microscope, Barnett also found seeds embedded in the blood that matched seeds found attached to the sock wrapped around Nancy's neck. A botanist from the University of California at Davis later matched these seeds to a plant that only grows in the Wooden Valley area, where Nancy's body was located.

After a five-week trial, Meneley was convicted of first-degree murder and sentenced to death. This was a rewarding conviction for Dick, although Menenley later appealed his conviction, claiming that this case and another criminal case involving him were improperly combined for prosecution. The appeal was denied, but his sentence was converted to life without the possibility of parole, due to recent court decisions that effectively outlawed the death penalty in California.

A second case that highlights Dick's ability to piece together evidence and leads involved one of the most bizarre and lesser-known murderers in Napa County's history. February 9, 1979, was a brisk morning. Just after sunrise, a motorist was driving on Buhman Avenue, a rural area dotted with vineyards and pastures just outside the border of Napa. As the motorist passed by a group of cows grazing in a field, his attention was draw to a dirt turn-out on the side of the road, where he saw the nude body of a man lying face down. The sheriff's department was immediately alerted, and Dick marshalled his fellow detectives to investigate. When Dick and crime scene investigator Hal Snook examined the body, they learned that the man had been shot three times—twice in the face and once in the back.

Detectives quickly identified the murdered man as Richard Niemeier. They tracked Niemeier's movements and learned that he lived in San Francisco and had last been seen in a gay bar in the SoMo (south of Market Street) area on the night before his body was found. Dick and his fellow detectives drove to San Francisco and spent several days interviewing patrons at gay bars and talking to people who knew Niemeier. Dick knew that tracing the movements of Niemeier in the days and hours leading up to his murder would be key to solving the case. Dick linked this case to a similar one that had been reported only four days before. In that case, on February 5, the partially nude body of Thomas Gloster had been found along a rural road in Tehama County. The links were undeniable—Gloster was last seen alive at the same bar as Niemeier, and they had both been shot multiple times. Within two weeks, ballistics tests on the shell casings found at both murder scenes conclusively linked them; Dick had a serial killer case on his hands.

Three months later and two states away, a man covered in blood staggered to a farmhouse in rural Pierce County, Washington. Deputies were called and found the man dazed and in shock—and that not all of the blood was his own. After medical aid and detectives were summoned, the story was pieced together. The man was a soldier at nearby Fort Lewis. He had been in downtown Tacoma visiting a friend when, hoping to get back to the base before curfew, he accepted a ride from a stranger in a black van. The driver, later identified as a Vietnam vet named Larry Hendricks, pulled out a pistol, made the man put on a black leather hood and handcuffed him. They drove to a wooded area, where Hendricks pulled the man from the van and began beating him with a billy club. Hendricks then half walked, half dragged the man deeper into the woods, prodding him with a shotgun and holding a pistol. He removed the man's hood and handcuffs.

Hendricks was clad in a black turtleneck and black leather pants and had a second pistol and the billy club tucked into his belt. At that point, the man noticed a headless torso on the ground nearby, and his flight-or-fight instincts kicked into overdrive. The man fought for his life, was able to wrestle the gun from Hendricks and shot him. Not taking any chances, the man grabbed a second pistol that Hendricks had tucked into his belt and emptied that gun into Hendricks's body. Still acting on adrenaline, anger and fear, the man grabbed the shotgun that Hendricks had brought and rammed the butt of it into Hendricks's face as he lay on the ground. The man ran back to the van and had enough presence of mind to remove an empty six-pack of beer and leave it on the roadside so that he could find the location again. He drove around aimlessly until he came to the rural farmhouse—the first sign of civilization. Deputies found the six-pack marker left and discovered Hendricks's lifeless body lying next to his last victim, another man Hendricks had kidnapped from Tacoma.

Dick detailed Detective John Robertson to fly to Tacoma and examine the evidence. Ballistics comparisons later confirmed that one of the guns found with Hendricks matched the one used to kill Niemeier and the Tehama County victim. The case file for one of Napa's strangest murderers was officially closed.

Dick's final Napa County Sheriff's Department identification card was issued to him in 2000. He retired two years later. *Courtesy of the Napa Police Historical Society.*

Dick went on to serve in positions of increasing responsibility in the sheriff's department, culminating in being appointed undersheriff by then sheriff Gary Simpson in 1994. The undersheriff runs the day-to-day operations of the sheriff's department. Dick retired in 2002.

Dick was involved in an astounding number of civic organizations and charities. In most of these organizations, he participated in some official capacity. He also taught for eighteen years in the Criminal Justice Program at Napa Valley College and served on the college's board of trustees.

In 2002, U.S. congressman Mike Thompson, on the floor of the 107th Congress, formally acknowledged Dick for his years of service to the citizens of Napa County. In 2008, Pope Benedict XVI imparted the Apostolic Blessing to Dick "in recognition for Ministry and Service for St. John the Baptist Catholic Church celebrating its 150th Anniversary and invokes an abundance of heavenly graces and the continued protection of the Blessed Virgin Mary." Dick passed away in 2015.

17

KEN JENNINGS

Kenneth Jennings was born in Silver City, Iowa, in 1931. The town was not much more than a whistle stop on the railroad in western Iowa and counted just over 350 residents when Ken lived there. Ken's father, Elmer, was a mechanic at the town's only repair shop. When Ken was in the first grade, his family moved out West with the flow of midwesterners fleeing the dustbowl. Ken later equated his early childhood to *The Grapes of Wrath*. In a time that predated interstates and minivans, the trip was arduous for the four adults and five children crammed into a single sedan. Ken was so excited when they finally reached their new home in Oakland that he jumped out of the car, kissed the ground and yelled, "Thank God for California!"

By 1942, Ken's family had settled in Atlas Peak, a mountain just northeast of Napa. Ken and his two younger sisters attended the local one-room schoolhouse.

In 1953, Ken was a student at Napa Junior College when he met and married fellow student and Napa native Virginia Jensen. The couple went on to have three daughters. His first job after college was as a fireman for the Napa Fire Department. Ken quickly figured out that his heart was not in it and decided he wanted to be a police officer instead.

Above: Ken Jennings's wooden baton was made of ironwood, a dense wood that ensured it would withstand the rigors of the job. *Courtesy of the Napa Police Historical Society.*

Officer Larry Antonini administers an early version of a polygraph examination to Ken during his hiring process in 1955. *Courtesy of the Napa Police Historical Society.*

Ken wanted to start working as a cop, but there were no openings in Napa, so he first pinned on a badge in the small town of Colusa, located in Yolo County, where he spent his first year. A spot finally opened at the Napa Police Department in 1955, and Ken happily returned to the town he considered home. Ken already had two connections to the Napa Police Department: two of his sisters were married to Napa police officers, Sherman Schulte and Bill Niles. Ken later joked that eventually both men wound up working for him.

Ken was given hand-me-down uniforms and was issued a .38-caliber Smith & Wesson revolver, handcuffs and a whistle. After spending six weeks at the police academy, his sergeant threw him a set of car keys and told him to go "10-8" (into service). At the time, there was no on-the-job field training program.

When interviewed as part of an oral history project in 2013, Ken described himself as the "last of the street walkers." He explained that he was the last officer assigned as a night watchman; his job was to walk around the downtown area rattling doors. Ken worked his way up the ranks, eventually becoming a sergeant.

Ken sits in the driver's seat of a patrol car in 1957, partnered with Reserve Officer Glenn Kingsford, in front of the police station on Fifth Street. *Courtesy of the Napa Police Historical Society.*

In 2011, the Napa Police Historical Society created a clone of the 1957 Ford that Ken drove as a young cop. He posed with the restored car in front of the former police station on Fifth Street, which is now a day spa. *Courtesy of the Napa Police Historical Society.*

When Chief Sherwood Munk died in 1967, it was a shock to everyone. It was a bit of a surprise and caused controversy when Ken was picked to replace Munk. At the time, Ken was only a sergeant; in fact, he was the most junior of the five sergeants at the department. There was an assistant chief and a captain who outranked him as well and had more time on the force. It turned out that the assistant chief and captain, Jack Blair and Art Corbett, were both nearing retirement and didn't want the job. Ken and two fellow sergeants were interviewed by a three-person panel consisting of the police chiefs from the cities of El Cerrito and South San Francisco, as well as a captain from the Berkeley Police Department.

Ken put out an acceptance statement to the media after being sworn in. It read in part, "I have devoted most of my adult years to law enforcement. I have chosen this way of life because I know that law enforcement is the basic way of ensuring our democratic way of life. I am convinced that without good law enforcement our way of life would be in dire jeopardy."

Ken continued the innovations started by Chief Munk and instituted others. He started by appointing several women as reserve officers in 1974 and then hired the first female Napa Police officer in 1978. Ken also expanded Chef Munk's efforts of connecting with the youth of Napa. Ken

Outgoing acting chief of police Jack Blair goes over paperwork with Ken after he was sworn in as chief in 1967. *Courtesy of the Napa Police Historical Society.*

started a program called Positive Image, where officers and support staff visit local high schools to speak to the students about law enforcement and drug abuse prevention, a precursor to the modern DARE program still taught in Napa schools.

Ken started many of the specialized units that have become integral parts of the police department, including the K-9 unit, the SWAT team and the cadet/explorer program. He looked for avenues to improve the effectiveness of the police department, including bringing in FBI agents to conduct advanced training and bringing in the international chief of police to conduct an assessment and offer suggestions.

When asked about the high point of his career during his oral history interview, Ken stated, "Having an honest department." If Ken learned that an officer lied in a report or lied to him during an internal investigation, that officer wasn't long for the department. Asked about regrets, Ken stated, "I don't have any. I wouldn't have changed a thing."

Ken was a strong supporter of the efforts of the Napa Police Historical Society to preserve the Napa Police Department's history. Early on, when I was just starting the NPHS, Ken invited me to his sprawling ranch on Second Avenue. He walked me to a barn and pulled a dusty box off an upper shelf. Ken rooted through the box and pulled out a handful of badges, most of which dated to the 1920s and 1930s. He also handed me a set of turn-of-the-century handcuffs that had come from Chief Nathaniel Boyd (featured in chapter 2). Ken graciously donated the badges and handcuffs to the fledgling history group.

During his retirement years, Ken enjoyed spending time with his family and friends, doting on his horses and riding his Harleys, woodworking, rock collecting, bird watching and spending time at his ranch property, located just east of Napa. Ken passed away suddenly at his home in 2014. Befitting Ken's love of all things country, his obituary contained the tagline "Happy trails…until we meet again." The Napa Police Historical Society was proud to park its restored 1957 Ford police car outside the funeral home—a final tribute to a man who left his mark on the history of the Napa Police Department.

18

K-9 VEM

The Napa Police Department K-9 program began in 1978. Officer John O'Donnell created the unit from scratch, building on the work that Napa County sheriff's deputy Dick Hathaway did the year prior when he secured the first K-9 in the county. John had worked for four years to put together the proposal to the city council, which eventually signed off on using $13,000 in federal revenue funds to purchase a dog and station wagon for use as a K-9 patrol car. O'Donnell conducted a thorough search for just the right dog, rejecting seventeen candidates before settling on a male German shepherd named November, who was quickly nicknamed Vem.

John and Vem went through a four-month police K-9 obedience training program in San Carlos, learning how to work together as a team. All of Vem's commands were in German, since he was imported from Europe as a puppy. This training is a crucial step in determining if a particular officer and K-9 partner can work together as an effective team. Just like any other

Above: This tombstone marked the final resting place of Napa Police K-9 Vem, who was killed in the line of duty in 1979. The tombstone bears a photograph of Vem and his handler, John O'Donnell. The tombstone was replaced, and this one was donated to the Napa Police Historical Society. *Courtesy of the Napa Police Historical Society.*

set of partners, at times personalities and temperaments don't mesh. The bond that forms is a close one and is necessary to ensure that the K-9 knows what the handler expects of it during the wide variety of calls that police handle. The K-9 becomes an extension of the handler. The bond extends past the work shift at the police department. K-9s live with the handlers and their families; when off duty, they become another family pet. In addition to their initial training, K-9s and their handlers participate in weekly training sessions to hone their skills.

Tragedy struck the police department's first K-9 team on July 1, 1979. They had been called to an apartment complex on Laurel Street, on the west side of Napa, for a report that a man named Harry Reece was going berserk and breaking the windows of cars parked at the complex. Before police arrived, Reece retreated into his apartment and locked the door. Several officers, including John and Vem, forced their way into the apartment, yelling for Reece to come out peacefully and give himself up. When no one answered, the officers started searching the small unit, and they found Reece hiding in a bedroom closet. Officers could see that Reece was armed with a knife, and John sent Vem to take him down. Unfortunately, Reece slashed at Vem, cutting the dog's throat. Officers quickly rushed in and tackled Reece, disarming him. Once Reece was detained, John scooped up Vem and rushed his stricken partner to a local animal hospital, where Vem underwent emergency surgery. Despite the valiant efforts of vets, Vem succumb to his injuries late that night.

Reece was held on a felony charge of assaulting a police officer. Outrage followed grief when Napa police officers learned that Reece had been released by a judge on his own recognizance. The judge didn't even make him post a bail. This was a slap in the face to officers, who saw Vem as a member of the Napa police family. What followed was a one-day "blue flu," in which every rank-and-file officer called in sick for their work shifts. The officers' spokesman, Vince Deguilio, told a local reporter, "We heard about an hour ago that Reece was ORd [released on his own recognizance] and we all became violently ill." The police chief scrambled to fill patrol shifts with his lieutenants and even strapped on a gun belt himself to help out.

The tragic death of Vem and the police officer's sick-out made national headlines. The mayor reported receiving phone calls from reporters seeking comments at his home in the middle of the night. The result was an outpouring of sympathy and support from people, both nationally and internationally. Stacks of cards and letters addressed to John arrived daily

Right: K-9 Vem posed for this photograph shortly after being deployed as the Napa Police Department's first K-9. He wears a custom Napa police badge hanging from his neck collar. *Courtesy of the Napa Police Historical Society.*

Below: Officer John O'Donnell and K-9 Vem pose with some of the trophies they won as a team during K-9 competitions in 1978 and 1979. Visible in the background is the station wagon that acted as the Napa Police Department's first K-9 vehicle. A door mat was taped to the top sill of the back door to help Vem grip while jumping out of the window. *Courtesy of the Napa Police Historical Society.*

K-9 Vem demonstrates his fearlessness during a jump over a five-foot-tall fence. Handler John O'Donnell can be seen in the background, peering over the fence. *Courtesy of the Napa Police Historical Society.*

at the police department. Many of these included monetary donations. The money was collected and donated to Napa's chapter of the Society for the Prevention of Cruelty to Animals (SPCA). This wound up being seed money for the SPCA's establishment of a spay and neuter clinic, which is still in operation today.

The bond that John formed with Vem was so close that he never sought a replacement K-9. Several other officers took over for John, and the K-9 unit was reformed in late 1979. Vem's sacrifice has not been forgotten. A plaque in honor of Vem hangs on the police department's Wall of Honor. Vem's name is also inscribed on the Faithful Partner K-9 memorial located at the Veterinary School of the University of California at Davis. The memorial lists all California K-9s killed in the line of duty.

The value of K-9 teams has been proven time and again. The K-9s used by Napa County law enforcement are all dual-purposes dogs, meaning they receive training in two disciplines. They are used during search operations to track and locate suspects. The dogs receive separate training to detect various narcotics, and they aid in vehicle and building searches, many times finding secreted drugs. Lastly, dogs receive training in patrol activities. Handlers can release a K-9 from a patrol car area by a remote control, and the dogs are

Officer John O'Donnell sits at the police department surrounded by cards and letters of support, which flooded in after Vem's killing in 1979. The donations received were donated to the local SPCA. *Courtesy of the Napa Police Historical Society.*

training to attack perceived threats or fleeing suspects when directed to do so by their handlers.

Since 1979, the Napa police K-9 unit has had two dogs at a time, which has remained the staffing level to this day. In addition, the Napa County Sheriff's Department employs six K-9 teams split between the contracted city of American Canyon and the sheriff's patrol itself.

19

NAPA CENTRAL DISPATCH

The earliest form of dispatching officers in Napa came in the form of red lights—not traffic signals, since these predated the first of those by at least half a century. These red lights were strung up at several key intersections in downtown Napa and were installed shortly after the city was electrified. As the police officer walked his beat, he could be alerted to the need for help when one of these lights was illuminated. The red light was a signal for the officer to hightail it back to the police station for an assignment. The lights were controlled by the desk sergeant, who stayed at the station waiting for trouble to be reported, either in person or via the department's lone telephone.

Until 1960, the job of dispatcher was handled during normal business hours by police clerk-dispatchers, all of whom were women. These women did double duty, handling the paperwork and filing duties of a clerk at the

Above: A key piece of equipment in the dispatch center for decades was this time clock stamp machine. Each emergency call dispatched to police and fire was tracked on a punch card, with the times of events printed on the card. This time clock was donated to the Napa Police Historical Society by the department in 2009. *Courtesy of the Napa Police Historical Society.*

police station and then grabbing the microphone when an officer needed to be called or called in and answering the emergency calls from citizens on the phone bank. A desk stacked high with radios and a telephone switchboard was nestled in a corner of the department's records bureau. At night and on weekends, a police officer or the sergeant would be assigned to sit at the station's dispatch center and fill in as dispatcher.

The Napa Police Department took its first steps toward forming a professional dispatch center in 1960, when it installed a switchboard and radio system in the basement of the police station. A female clerk was assigned to answer the telephones and police radio full-time from 10:00 a.m. until 6:00 p.m. After hours, dispatching and phone calls were still taken care of by on-duty patrol officers.

In 1961, the Napa Police Department appointed its first two male clerk-dispatchers and assigned them to work the off-hours, freeing up the police officers. One of these was Hal Snook, who went on to have a long career at the Napa County Sheriff's Department and is the subject of chapter 15. Eventually, the job of clerk-dispatcher was split.

Undoubtedly, the most famous emergency call to ever be received at the Napa Police Department came in at 7:40 p.m. on the night of December 20, 1968. At that time, the normal dispatcher was on a break, and Officer Dave Slaight was tapped to man the phones and radio. More than likely, Dave was the junior man on duty that night, since this is the typical duty for a rookie or low man on the totem pole. Dave answered the phone to hear a calm man say, "I want to report a murder, no, a double murder. They are two miles north of Park Headquarters. They were in a white Volkswagen Karmann Ghia." The phone call was traced to a payphone in downtown Napa, but the killer was gone by the time officers arrived at the phone booth. Thus Dave became one of only two people to ever hear the voice of the infamous Zodiac killer.

In 1979, Napa police dispatchers combined with their counterparts at the Napa County Sheriff's Department. They became county employees and physically moved to the sheriff's office. Some Napa police dispatchers were leery because their counterparts were paid $200 less per month, but the guarantee of pay parity smoothed matters over. The police and sheriffs determined that combining their dispatch centers would save $50,000 a year. This arrangement lasted ten years and ended when a new dispatch center was constructed at the police station. Since that time, the Napa Central Dispatch Center has been staffed by police employees. The center dispatches for the Napa Police, Napa Sheriff,

Napa police officer Frank Madalena sits at the dispatch area of the police station in 1959. *Courtesy of the Napa Police Historical Society.*

Napa police dispatcher Etta Crocker is shown in the dispatch center, which was in the basement of the police station, in 1973. *Courtesy of the Napa Police Historical Society.*

This 1987 photograph shows the Napa Central Dispatch Center when it was located at the Napa County Sheriff's Department. Pictured are Theresa Kramer (*left*) and Carolynn Jolliffe. *Courtesy of the Napa Police Historical Society.*

Napa Fire Department, American Canyon Fire Protection District and AMR ambulance service.

A 1987 article about the dispatch center put it this way: "The police and sheriff's deputies in Napa County may be the long arm of the law, but the Central Dispatch Center is its brain-center." I can speak from my own experience that police officers rely heavily on the dispatchers and the information that they glean from callers, who often are upset or in shock. Without the detailed information obtained, we would literally be driving into situations blind.

In addition, dispatchers are responsible for obtaining medical information from and providing instructions on first aid to frantic callers. The information they obtain from these calls helps inform the fire department and ambulance personnel on what type of response they will initiate and which resources to send to a particular call. After gleaning crucial details, dispatchers then coordinate the emergency response, monitoring the rapidly changing events that field units encounter and ensuring that everyone stays on the same page.

Perhaps the greatest change in dispatching since the advent of 911 as the catch-all emergency phone number happened in December 2009, when

Napa dispatchers pose for a feature newspaper article in 1993. The article focused on how dispatchers can save lives by the first aid and CPR instruction they give over the phone to panicked 911 callers. Dispatchers pictured are (*left to right*): Kelli Lyerla, Bev Turner and Charlene Everett. *Courtesy of the Napa Police Historical Society.*

the dispatch center began taking 911 calls from cellular phones. Prior to that time, all the cellular calls were automatically routed to the California Highway Patrol's regional dispatch center. From that time on, calls came to Napa's dispatch center if they originated in an area away from the highway, based on cellular tower connection data. This change greatly increased the workload in the dispatch center, due to erroneously dialed 911 calls, colloquially known as butt dials. This problem has only grown as the pervasiveness of cellular devices in society has.

In 2003, the dispatch center underwent a major remodel, upgrading the workstations to state-of-the-art computer terminals and ergonomic desks that allowed dispatchers to stand if they wanted to. In 2006, yet another upgrade to the center was performed, this time allowing the computer-aided dispatching to integrate with the use of newly installed in-vehicle mobile data computers (MDCs) and real-time tracking of emergency vehicle locations (GPS). Today the demands on dispatchers have expanded with the dispatch center receiving 911 calls from cellular devices and will be further tested when the next upgrade to the wireless 911 system, known as Next Gen 911, goes live. Dispatchers will be receiving more accurate GPS data on cell phone locations and will start accepting 911 calls from text message or even texted images and videos. As technology progresses so do the demands on dispatchers and their ability to multitask.

20

NAPA POLICE SWAT

The term "SWAT" has become an acronym known to many, yet what it stands for and the job of the units that hold this designation are not well understood by the general public. SWAT stands for Special Weapons and Tactics. The first SWAT teams were formed in Philadelphia and Los Angeles in the early 1960s, in response to a series of violent bank robberies and riots. During this time, patrol officers were typically armed with six-shot revolvers and sometimes a pump-action shotgun mounted in their vehicle.

The first Napa Police Department SWAT team was formed in 1978, two years after the Napa County Sheriff's Department formed a team. The first NPD team consisted of the only five officers who passed the physical test. Besides the mile and a half run, pull-ups and sit-ups, the final test was a twenty-five-foot hands-only rope climb at Napa High School's

Above: This tiger-striped camouflage uniform shirt belonged to inaugural Napa Police Department SWAT team member Vince Deguilio. The uniform didn't employ camouflaged or subdued colored shoulder patches, but instead used the standard patches worn by all officers at the time. *Courtesy of the Napa Police Historical Society.*

gym. The story goes that the chief at the time, Ken Jennings, had hand-picked several officers to be on the SWAT team, and quite a few officers tried out; however, as officers took turns at the rope, potential candidates (including all of the chief's picks) failed. The administration started to grow concerned that no one would pass, but five did, and they became the first team. They were Vince Deguilio, Ruben Faria, Randy Bowman, Gary Simpson and Bruce Baker.

The first team went to an army surplus store on Couch Street in Vallejo to buy their initial mix-and-match used equipment. One team member who was a combat veteran even wore the boots he brought back from the Vietnam War. The team didn't have a shoulder patch at all; instead, they had an embroidered badge patch that was made locally. Their initial uniforms were surplus tiger-striped pattern camouflage.

The first Napa Police Department SWAT team posed for this 1978 photograph while attending FBI training at Hamilton Air Force Base in the nearby city of Novato. Pictured are (*left to right*): Ruben Faria, Bruce Baker, Vince Deguilio, Randy Bowman and Gary Simpson. *Courtesy of the Napa Police Historical Society.*

Since there was no budget for team equipment, a police rangemaster at the time sold a fully automatic Thompson sub-machine gun in the armory to fund the purchase five M-16 military-style assault rifles. When the chief found out about the unauthorized sale, he ordered the rangemaster to retrieve the Thompson or be fired. Luckily for his career, the rangemaster was able to get it back. Later, under a different chief of police, the Thompson was traded for five suppressed MP-5 machine guns for the team.

The first team attended a one-week training session with the Federal Bureau of Investigations at the Los Guilicos Training Center in Sonoma County. Later, the team received ongoing training from the FBI, which trained many of the SWAT teams in the Bay Area at the time. The FBI rotated the training to various federal facilities throughout the Bay Area, such as the decommissioned Hamilton Air Force Base in nearby Marin County. Examples of training included rappelling inside aircraft hangers, building searches and the use of BB guns for force-on-force scenario training. The early SWAT team did not coordinate with the Napa sheriff's SWAT team. They only occasionally saw each other at FBI-sponsored training.

In 1980, a second group of SWAT members were added; they also made the drive to Couch Street for equipment and uniforms. They picked out whatever would fit, and there was no real match in design. Some had the old tiger-stripe camouflage uniforms like team one, with others had woodland camouflage pattern uniforms.

This team's first training was at Hamilton Air Force Base with the FBI. There was a local news crew filming at the base. When they drove out after their last day of training, a team member threw a string of firecrackers at the film crew. The team then beat a hasty retreat, driving in an unmarked undercover car. A team member recalled that whoever was driving floored the gas and they sped away as fast as a four-cylinder Plymouth could manage, hitting a top speed of twenty-five or thirty miles per hour as they turned the corner.

The team stopped at a Round Table Pizza just outside the base. A team member produced a firecracker, and he pulled the fuse halfway out, thinking it would not cause the firecracker to explode. He lit it and then threw it on the table among several pitchers of beverages. He was laughing joyously as several of the team members attempted to swat out the fuse. The firecracker fell between cracks in slats in the table and exploded under the table. His exuberant expression quickly turned to one of shock. The pizza parlor manager ran to the table and yelled that he was going to call

The original Napa Police Department SWAT team reunited in 2018. They posed at the same location as they did in the 1978 photograph, at the now-defunct Hamilton Air Force Base. *Courtesy of the Napa Police Historical Society.*

the Novato Police for shooting guns in the restaurant. Since the team was clad in military camo, a member quickly told the manager that they were a detachment from the nonexistent Fifty-First Marines that had just returned from overseas and assured the manager that he would keep a close eye on the team, and there would be no further problems. He was able to calm the manager, and there were no more firecracker tricks. According to a team member, that was actually one of the tamer after-training sessions they had.

The first Napa SWAT patch was created in 1986. Recognizing the need for a subdued SWAT patch, two sergeants, Bill Jabin and Gary Domingo, drove to a trophy shop in Santa Rosa that did patches for local bowling teams. With a rough conceptual draft of a patch shaped like the Butte County Sheriff's Office, the SWAT patch was born. The SWAT uniform was also standardized to the woodland camouflage pattern. The initial patch was used until 1989, when it was replaced by a subdued version of the standard NPD patch.

Members of the SWAT team have carried on the tradition of repurposing surplus gear beyond the old Vietnam-era clothing they snagged at the surplus store in Vallejo. The first full-time SWAT vehicle at the Napa Police Department was a repurposed bank armored car, acquired from a Southern California company in 1997. Later, in 2014, the SWAT team was able to acquire a surplus mine-resistant ambush-resistant vehicle (MRAP) from the military. There was a quantity of these vehicles returning from service in Iraq and Afghanistan, and they were offered free to local law enforcement. Although the MRAP was infinitely better than the old armored car, it was still not purpose-built for law enforcement, and it spurred a series of discussions about the militarization of the police. Early in 2020, the SWAT team finally purchased an armored vehicle built with the needs and demands of civilian law enforcement in mind.

One of the most interesting SWAT callouts happened in April 2014 in a remote area of nearby Sonoma County. The case started several days before in Napa, when a love triangle resulted in one of the involved men shooting up the car of his competition, with the owner in it. Unbelievably, the man in the car wasn't hit, though his car wasn't so lucky, as evidenced by the bullet holes officers found in the hood and inside a flattened front tire. The suspect, Mauricio Tovar-Telles, was quickly identified, and detectives set up a stakeout later that night at a house where he was supposed to show up. An officer saw the car pass by and pulled it over. Tovar-Telles was found hiding in the back seat, a gun tucked into the folds of the seat. Ballistics would later confirm that the gun was used in the drive-by shooting. Detectives questioned Tovar-Telles, and he identified a friend named Miguel Angel Garcia as the person who gave him the gun used in the shooting.

The first Napa Police Department SWAT team patch unique to the unit was created by Sergeants Bill Jabin and Gary Domingo in 1986. *Courtesy of the Napa Police Historical Society.*

The next day, agents from Napa's special investigations bureau took over the case. They had an open investigation into Garcia, and he already had an arrest warrant for unrelated narcotics and weapons charges. They went to a mobile home in rural Sonoma County after Tovar-Telles said that was where Garcia was holed up. The Sonoma County SWAT team was called in, as well as a crisis negotiations team from Napa and Sonoma Counties. What resulted was a hostage standoff, with Garcia preventing a woman acquaintance from leaving. During the standoff crisis, negotiators opened a

The Napa Police Department SWAT team poses with its newly acquired armored car in 1997. When the department received the vehicle, it was repainted, and emergency lights and a siren were added. *Courtesy of the Napa Police Historical Society.*

dialogue with Garcia via phone. They were shocked when Garcia confessed that he had kidnapped a man in Santa Rosa and, with Tovar-Telles's help, murdered him in a rural area of Napa County.

The Napa Police SWAT team relieved the Sonoma County team late in the day. This is a common practice, allowing teams to get rest while maintaining a perimeter. Garcia died during an exchange of gunfire with SWAT members after he walked out of the mobile home early on the second day of the standoff. The next day, Tovar-Telles admitted to helping Garcia dispose of a body in Napa County and led detectives to the grave site.

Today the Napa Police SWAT team consists of twelve members. Ancillary teams of tactical dispatchers, crisis negotiators and fire department medics work with the team as needed. Prospective new members must pass the same physical agility test given to FBI SWAT team members, with the exception that Napa officer candidates must complete the run fifteen seconds faster than the FBI standard. Candidates also sit for an oral board interview. Once invited to join the team, new members must attend and pass a two-week SWAT school certified by the California Commission on Peace Officer Standards and Training (POST). The NPD SWAT team is not a full-time assignment, but team members are called in as needed for critical incidents and planned operations. They also can use their skills and knowledge to benefit the various bureaus where they are assigned within the department, donning gear and acting alone or in small numbers as a quick reaction force until the full SWAT team can be called in and deployed.

21

THE NAPA POLICE
FOOTBALL TEAM

Some say that police work is a contact sport. In many ways, being a police officer is like being a player on a football team. Each position relies on other team members for support, and no one player can succeed without his or her teammates. The fact is that every law enforcement agency has a minimum physical agility standard and testing for new officers, and physical fitness is an important part of being an officer.

For years, local officers competed in individual sport by participating in annual Police and Fire Olympic events, both in California and nationally. The Napa Police Department's first foray into organized sports came in 1970, when the department fielded a basketball team to play against a

Above: This jersey was worn by the police officers during noncontact practices and was offered to the wives of the officers who played on the football team. The number noted at the center of the jersey matched the player number of their husbands. *Courtesy of the Napa Police Historical Society.*

Napa sheriff's team in a charity game. The team captains were Chief of Police Ken Jennings and Napa County sheriff Earl Randol. In 1978, the department's athletic endeavors went to the next level, when a full-contact football team was formed.

The roots of the football team were planted in 1976, when two Napa Fire Department firefighters named Jon Trebotich and Steve Ceriani saw a newspaper article about Sacramento's Pig Bowl, a charity football game that pitted the Sacramento County sheriffs against the Sacramento police. It took two years for Jon and Steve to convince the local police and fire unions, and their members, to strap on their cleats. The final hurdle of securing the venue, Napa's Memorial Stadium, didn't happen until four weeks before the planned game.

The inaugural game was held at Memorial Stadium, the football venue that was shared by both local public high schools, Napa and Vintage High Schools. The police team was officially organized by the officer's union, the Napa Police Officers Association (NPOA). Its opponent was the Napa City Firefighter's Association (NCFA). From the beginning, the police team's ranks were thin. There were only fifty-two men on the force at the time, and not all of those were ready to strap on pads and helmets. The officers recruited several Napa County sheriff's deputies to help fill out the team. Likewise, the Napa Fire Department augmented its ranks with several firefighters from other agencies within the county. The police team tapped several coaches and staff members from the Napa Valley Bears, a semipro team in the California Football League, to whip them into shape. What ensued was a series of practices to build a team and knock the rust off the players, many of whom hadn't worn helmets and pads since their glory days of high school.

No good football game would be complete without cheerleaders, and a group of female employees at the Napa Police Department created a cheer squad. They enlisted the help of a couple of recently graduated high school cheerleaders who happened to be the daughters of police officers to help create the routines. The cheerleaders donned blue and yellow uniforms, matching the colors of the team they were rooting for.

With everything finally in place, the charity game was held in November 1978. Over four thousand tickets were sold, with the proceeds split four ways between the athletic programs of Napa and Vintage High Schools and the police and fire unions. The sharing of raised funds with the schools was key to securing the use of Memorial Stadium. Although the firefighters soundly defeated the cops, 14-0, both teams vowed to come back next year, and an annual tradition was born.

The 1980 Napa police football team. *Courtesy of the Napa Police Historical Society.*

Members of the Napa police football team on the sidelines during the 1979 game. *Courtesy of D. Bruce Miller.*

Not to be left out, some female employees at the police department banded together to form a cheer squad. The police cheer squad performs during half-time at the 1979 game. *Courtesy of D. Bruce Miller.*

For the first four years, the annual football game pitted police versus fire. The police team's record wasn't the greatest, 0-3-1, but they made up for the lack of wins with tenacity and spirit. In 1982, the police team branched out and participated in two games. The first was against a team from nearby Solano County law enforcement agencies in what was dubbed the first-annual Wine Valley Bowl. For the second, the team traveled all the way to Salinas in the central valley of California to pay a game against the Monterey County Mounties law enforcement team in a game known locally as the Bacon Bowl.

In 1983, Napa fielded a joint team known as the Napa County Peace Officers. The name was a bit of a misnomer, since by this time the team actually consisted of both law enforcement (Napa Police, Napa Sheriff, St. Helena Police, Calistoga Police, Napa County Department of Corrections and California Highway Patrol) and five firefighters from the Napa City Fire Department and California Department of Forestry. The team's nickname was the Stompers. They played what turned out to be their final game against a Santa Rosa police team.

The death knell for the football team was injuries. Too many officers were getting hurt on the gridiron and then were not able to work their regular

Left: The souvenir program from the 1980 police versus fire football game. The program features caricatures of animals associated with police officers and firefighters: a pig and a dalmatian. *Courtesy of the Napa Police Historical Society.*

Below: Stephanie and Dan Lonergan at the 1980 football game. Stephanie sports one of the spouse jerseys. *Courtesy of the Napa Police Historical Society.*

jobs, much to the chagrin of the top brass at the involved departments. The injured included the police team's star running back, Dan Lonergan, who hurt his neck. When I surveyed former players for this book, several also mentioned age as a factor. These reasons parallel why many in public safety can't complete a full career. As officers get older, the people they chase are seemingly always being replaced with young criminals. Police and fire personnel are plagued by injuries related to their job and the equipment they must carry.

Although the era of football heroes was gone, the love of sport did not die at the Napa Police Department. A flag football team continued to play for several years, as did a softball team. Later, in the 2010s, the police department formed a basketball team and played several charity games against the Napa Fire Department, titled Hoops to Prevent Youth Violence, with the proceeds benefiting a mentorship program for at-risk high schoolers. A softball team also formed and played in a tournament for public safety teams from around the region, called the Heroes of the Valley, which raised funds for the police department's youth services bureau.

BIBLIOGRAPHY

Books

Allen, Charles H., and R.E. Wood. *Life and Confessions of James Gilbert Jenkins, the Murderer of Eighteen Men.* San Francisco: William P. Harrison & Company, 1864.

Chamberlain, William H., and Harry L. Wells. *History of Sutter County, California.* Oakland, CA: Thompson and West, 1879.

Eighmey, Rae Katherine. *Soda Shop Salvation: Recipes and Stores from the Sweeter Side of Prohibition.* Minneapolis: Minnesota Historical Society, 2013.

Gregory, Thomas Jefferson. *History of Solano and Napa Counties California.* Los Angeles: Historical Research Company, 1912.

Guadagni, Raymond A. *The Adventures of the Squeezebox Kid.* Kingston Springs, TN: Westview Publishing, 2016.

Irvine, Leigh H. *A History of the New California: Its Resources and People.* Vol 2. New York: Lewis Publishing, 1905.

Napa Police Department Souvenir. Napa, CA: Semorile Printing Company, 1913.

Palmer, Lyman L. *History of Napa and Lake Counties California.* San Francisco: Slocum, Bowen and Company, 1881.

Shulman, Todd L. *Murder and Mayhem in the Napa Valley.* Charleston, SC: The History Press, 2012.

Street, Richard Steven. *Beasts of the Field: A Narrative History of California Farmworkers, 1769–1913.* Palo Alto, CA: Stanford University Press, 2004.

Sullivan, Russell. *Rocky Marciano: The Rock of His Times.* Champaign: University of Illinois Press, 2002.

Newspapers

Clovis News Journal. "Clovis Taxi Driver Victim of Two Kidnapers." February 22, 1935.

————. "Five-Year-Old Clovis Kidnaping Solved by G-Men." February 9, 1941.

Napa Daily Register. "Alex Herritt Is Appointed Police Chief by the Mayor." September 23, 1922.

————. "Brother Beats Police Officer." August 8, 1936.

————. "City Shocked by Sudden Death of Police Chief." January 26, 1933.

————. "Friends Give Gold Star to Chief Herritt." August 25, 1930.

————. "Girls Identify Wounded Suspect." June 17, 1933.

————. "Last Honors Accorded Late Police Chief A.F. Herritt." January 27, 1933.

————. "Napa Police Stage Raid Last Night." May 30, 1931.

————. "N.E. Boyd, Former Napa Chief Police, Summoned." January 15, 1925.

————. "Police Chief Alex. Herritt Dead." January 25, 1933.

————. September 11, 1925.

————. "Stone House Is Raided; No Arrests Made as Yet." December 2, 1924.

Napa Journal. "Burglar Suspect in Jail Here Held for FBI on Kidnaping Charges." February 8, 1941.

————. "Crosby is taken to Sacramento by U.S. Marshals." February 15, 1941.

————. "Geo. D. Secord Passed Away Yesterday." June 1, 1927.

————. "Three Suspects Held Here After Burglary Attempt at Napa Steam Laundry." January 3, 1941.

Napa Register. "Bank Holdup. Robber Wanted Money for Woman Friend's Christmas." December 9, 1958.

————. "Benefit Football Game Huge Success." December 2, 1978.

————. "Body of Woman Found Draped over Bath Tub." November 15, 1965.

————. "Central Dispatch: Pros and Cons." March 15, 1979.

————. "CHP Officer Critchley Paid Tribute at Retirement Fete." January 13, 1969.

————. "City Initiates First Step Toward Major Communications Center; Police Switch Made." June 29, 1960.

————. "C.J. Madalena." June 23, 1963.

————. "Delph Rood Rexroth." January 19, 1981.

————. "Details on Finding Body Opens Trial." May 6, 1970.

————. "Edward J. Glos." April 4, 1972.

———. "Finding on Body Enters into Trial." May 27, 1970.

———. "Fire Blanks Police." December 30, 1979.

———. "Five Napans Killed in Crash." August 5, 1957.

———. "Hal Snook Retiring: He'll Do Things He Missed." May 2, 1980.

———. "Jennings Is New Police Chief." August 28, 1967.

———. June 3, 1967.

———. "Jurors Asked to Find Meneley Guilty of Murder as Final Arguments Given by District Attorney." June 4, 1970.

———. "Latest Rookie Cop a Real Dog at Work." May 19, 1978.

———. "Looking into Napa's Past and Present." April 24, 1972.

———. "Marciano Given Tremendous Reception at Calistoga." April 4, 1955.

———. "Mel Critchley, Badge No. 1 CHP Officer, Dies at 74." June 19, 1980.

———. "Melvin Critchley Retiring from CHP." December 19, 1968.

———. "Meneley Found Guilty; Murder in 1st Degree." June 10, 1970.

———. "A Misty Goodbye to Mae's." November 9, 1978.

———. "Murdered Man Found in Napa Area." February 9, 1979.

———. "Mysterious Hatchet Murder in Napa." January 15, 1980.

———. "Napa Lawmen Return to Streets After Protest." July 4, 1979.

———. "Napa Man Charged in Killing." October 16, 1969.

———. Napa's Past & Present. February 12, 1972.

———. Napa's Past & Present. October 30, 1971.

———. "Narlow Retires After 28 Years." October 17, 1987.

———. November 9, 1961.

———. "Police Inspector Rexroth to Retire after 22 Years of Law Enforcement Work." June 18, 1964.

———. "Police Mourn Death of Vem." July 2, 1979.

———. "Ralph Madalena Dies as Kin Race East to Side." December 12, 1955.

———. "Same Gun Used for Napa and Tehama Deaths." February 22, 1979.

———. "Services for Chief Munk Set Friday." June 1, 1967.

———. "Shotgun Blast Kills Napa Police Chief." May 31, 1967.

———. "Someone Who's There When You Need Them." July 9, 1993.

———. "Stompers Physically Prepared for Wine Bowl." August 19, 1983.

———. "That Was Napa." October 9, 1963.

———. "Upvalley Man Held in Murder of PUC Coed." March 17, 1971.

———. "Vem's Death Makes National Headlines." July 3, 1979.

———. "Veteran Sergeants Retiring." December 13, 1983.

———. "Williams Found Guilty; 1st Degree." July 23, 1971.

Napa Valley Register. "Are Napa's Law Enforcement Agencies Militarized or Thrifty?" August 23, 2014.

———. "Armored Car Gives Napa Cops Added Security." December 22, 1997.

———. "Charles A. Hansen Jr." June 1, 2006.

———. "Harold Snook." April 14, 2010.

———. "Ken Jennings." June 5, 2014.

———. "Tracking the Mark of the Zodiac for Decades." February 18, 2007.

———. "Zodiac Killer Case Investigator Dies of Cancer." December 2, 2010.

Napa Weekly Register. "New Rules: Napa Now Has Two Regular Patrolmen." July 9, 1909.

Press-Democrat. "Man Killed in Kenwood Standoff Was Napa Fugitive." April 4, 2014.

———. "When the Champ, Rocky Marciano, came to Calistoga." May 2, 2015.

St. Helena Star. "Chinaman Shot." September 18, 1885.

———. "A Free Man." October 16, 1885.

———. "The Town Election." April 15, 1876.

Weekly Calistogan. "Local Bank Robber Caught in Eight-Minute Chase." December 11, 1958.

Online Resources

"California, County Marriages, 1850–1952." Family Search. www.familysearch.org.

"Iowa, World War II Bonus Case Files, 1947–1954." Ancestry. Ancestry.com.

"John Hall Allison." St. Helena Historical Society. https://www.shstory.org.

NPD Football Player Survey. SurveyMonkey Inc. March 30, 2019.

Unpublished Works

Jennings, Ken oral history interview with author. Napa, CA. March 14, 2013.

Munk, Ruth oral history interview with author. Napa, CA. June 2, 2006.

O'Neill, Doug. The History of the Calistoga Police Department.

Scribner, Bani oral history interview with author. Sacramento, CA. December 17, 2006.

ABOUT THE AUTHOR

Todd L. Shulman is a California native who has worked in law enforcement his entire adult life; he began as a military police person in the U.S. Army, serving in Iraq during the First Gulf War. Later Shulman returned to California and became a police officer; he recently retired from the Napa Police Department. He has held numerous positions in the police department, including sergeant, detective, training officer, crime scene specialist, corporal and cold case investigator. Shulman formed the non-profit Napa Police Historical Society in 2006 and continues today as its president. Shulman has written three other books, all chronicling various aspects of Napa history. Besides his focus on history, Shulman volunteers his time raising funds for Special Olympics through the Law Enforcement Torch Run. Shulman is married and has two adult sons who just finished college.

Visit us at
www.historypress.com